*To all the artisans
from the Eastern Townships region*

Canadian Cataloguing in Publication Data

Foreman, Michèle
    Flavours of a region Eastern Townships

Photos: Michèle Foreman
    Except for photo page 13 – Vaillancourt Family

Photographs were taken outdoors, without artifice
to modify food appearance.

ISBN 978-2-9808183-7-0

Legal Deposit – Bibliothèque nationale du Québec, 2007
Legal Deposit – National Library of Canada, 2007

All rights reserved. No part of this publication may be reproduced or transmitted
without the prior permission of the author or as expressly permitted by law.

Printed in Quebec

Also available in French:
    L'histoire savoureuse d'une région Outaouais – 2003
    L'histoire savoureuse d'une région Bas-Saint-Laurent – 2004
    L'histoire savoureuse d'une région Québec – 2004
    L'histoire savoureuse d'une région Chaudière-Appalaches – 2005
    L'histoire savoureuse d'une région Cantons-de-l'Est – 2007

From the same author:
    Savour Quebec Regional Bounty – 2005

www.stellaireediteur.com

TABLE OF CONTENTS

Foreword 7

The Magnificent Eastern Townships 9

The Story of the Land 10

Keepers of Time 12

Artisan Producers 15

Backroad Treasures 27

Chefs and Innkeepers 36

Recipes 49

Acknowledgements 115

Recipes Index 117

Producers' Addresses 123

Restaurants and Inns 125

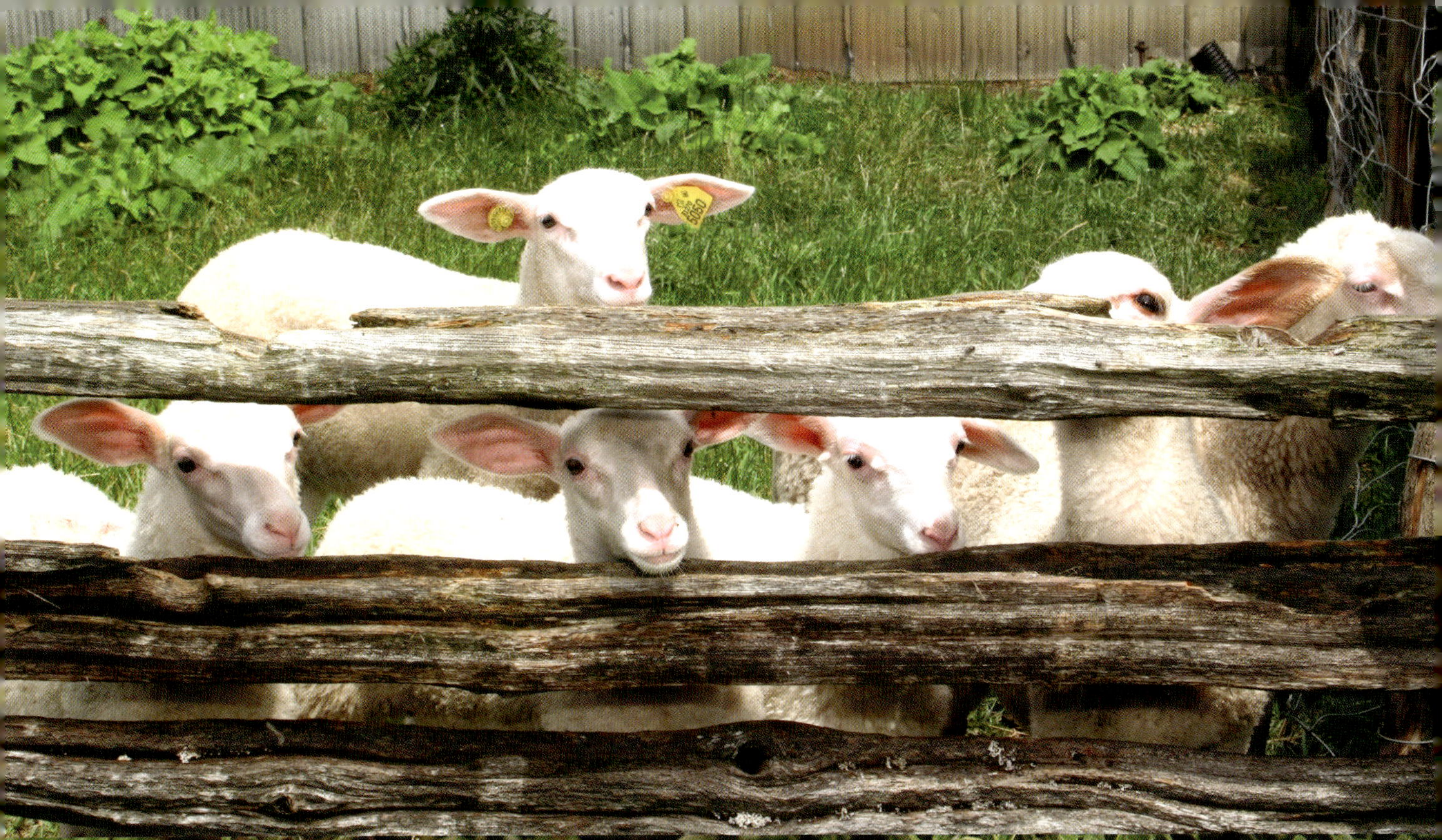

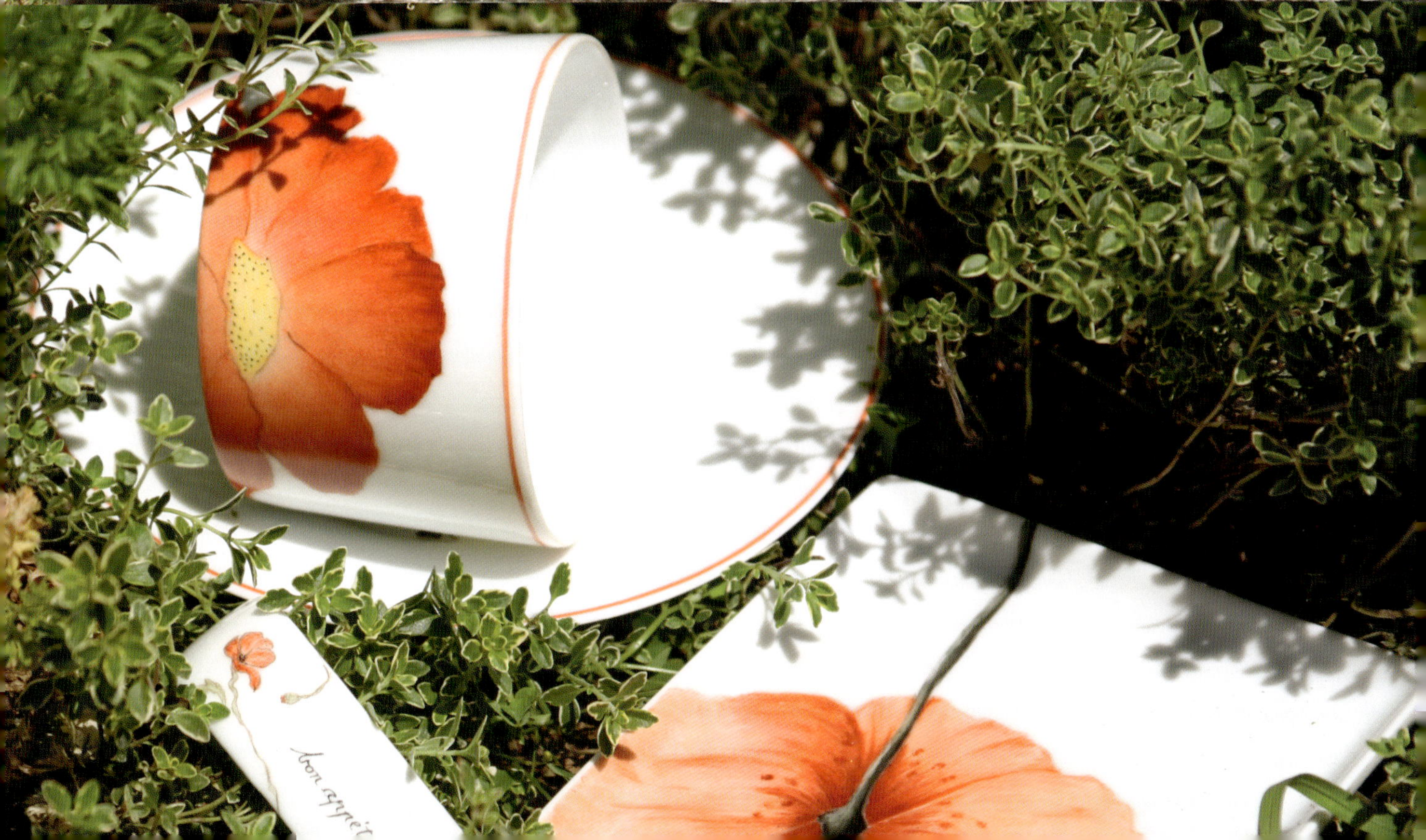

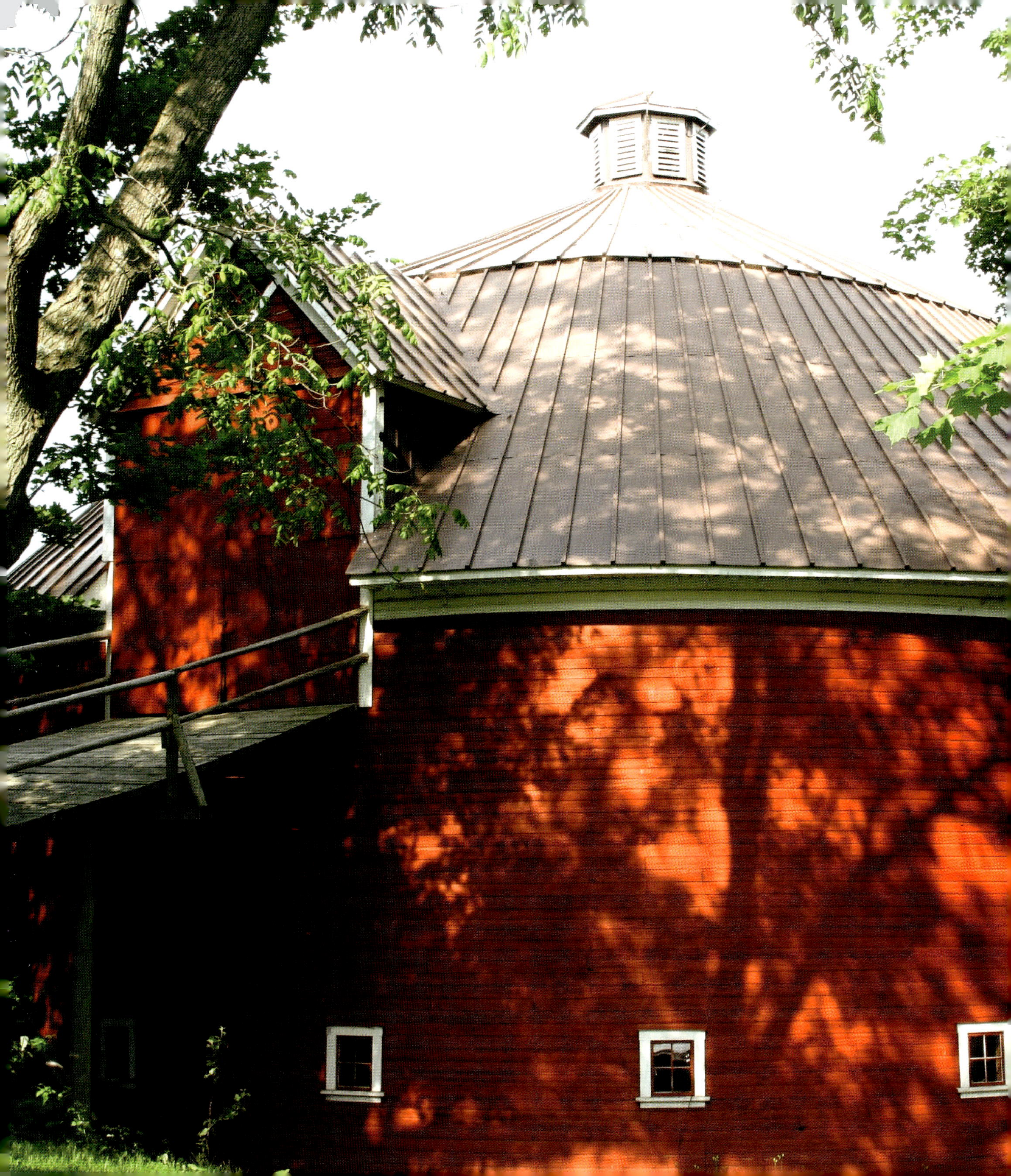

Foreword

Please join me for a drive along the backroads of the beautiful Eastern Townships region, a veritable treasure chest!

In particular, come and meet the producers and chefs, artisans who work with a rich palette of colours, aromas, and flavours. Their eagerness to share the details and delights of their occupations with others testifies to the immense pride they take in their work.

Farming specialties, traditional food and wines, inns, small cafés, fairs, and farmers' markets—every attraction is a new opportunity to savour the considerable diversity of local products, whether duck or goat, cheese or alcoholic berry drinks, all lovingly bred or processed by local residents for your pleasure.

The Eastern Townships are all that and much more. The people from around here—in the workshops, fields, apple groves, and vineyards—have built this region, and they deserve our admiration. I hope that you will join me in paying homage to the conviction, perseverance, concern for tradition, and talents of these producers and chefs, who constantly find new ways to delight.

Allow yourself the pleasure of coming to meet these men and women, and hear their stories firsthand. Learn about their region, trades, values, products, and land. You will come away much richer for it.

And may all your discoveries be delicious!

Joyeuses gourmandises!

Michèle Foreman

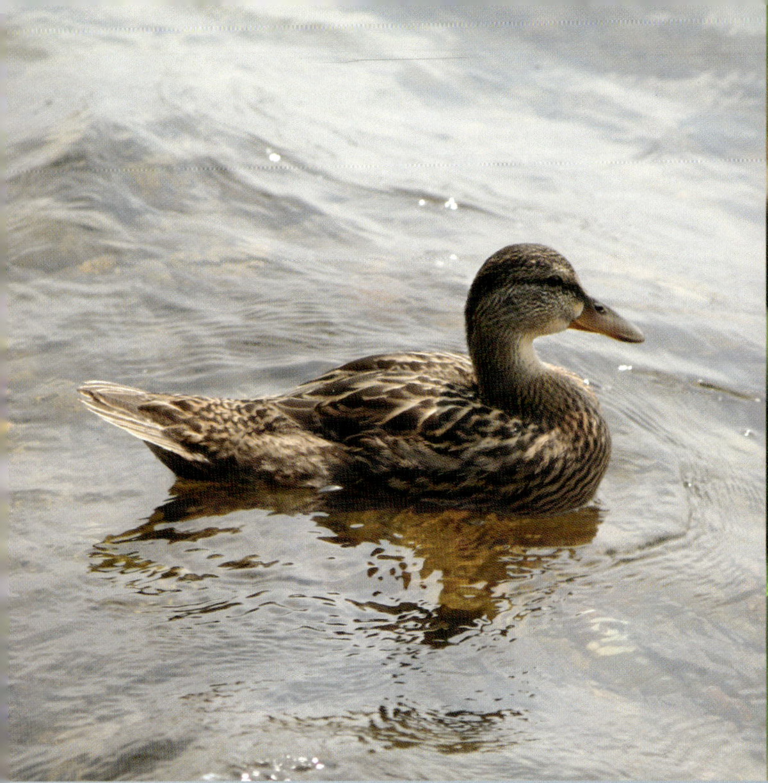
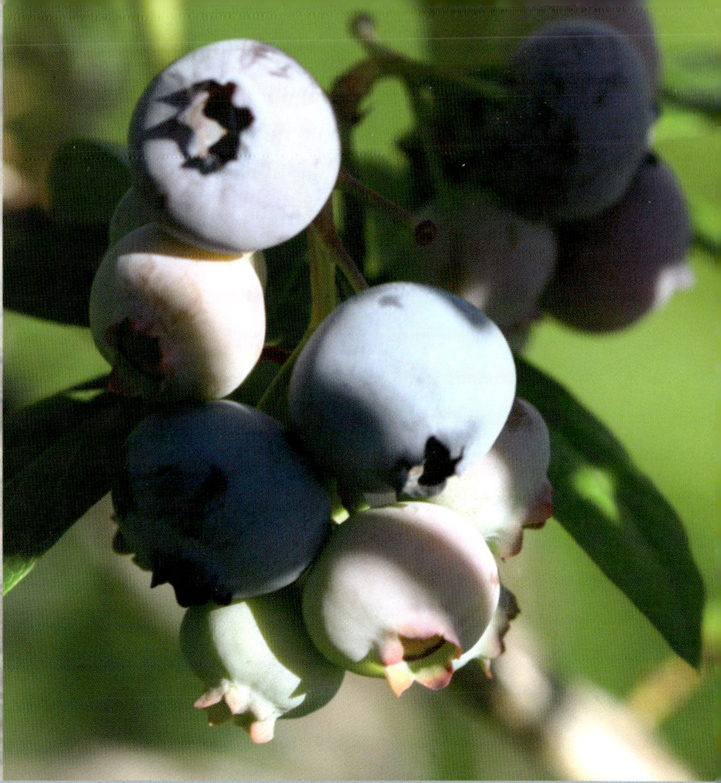
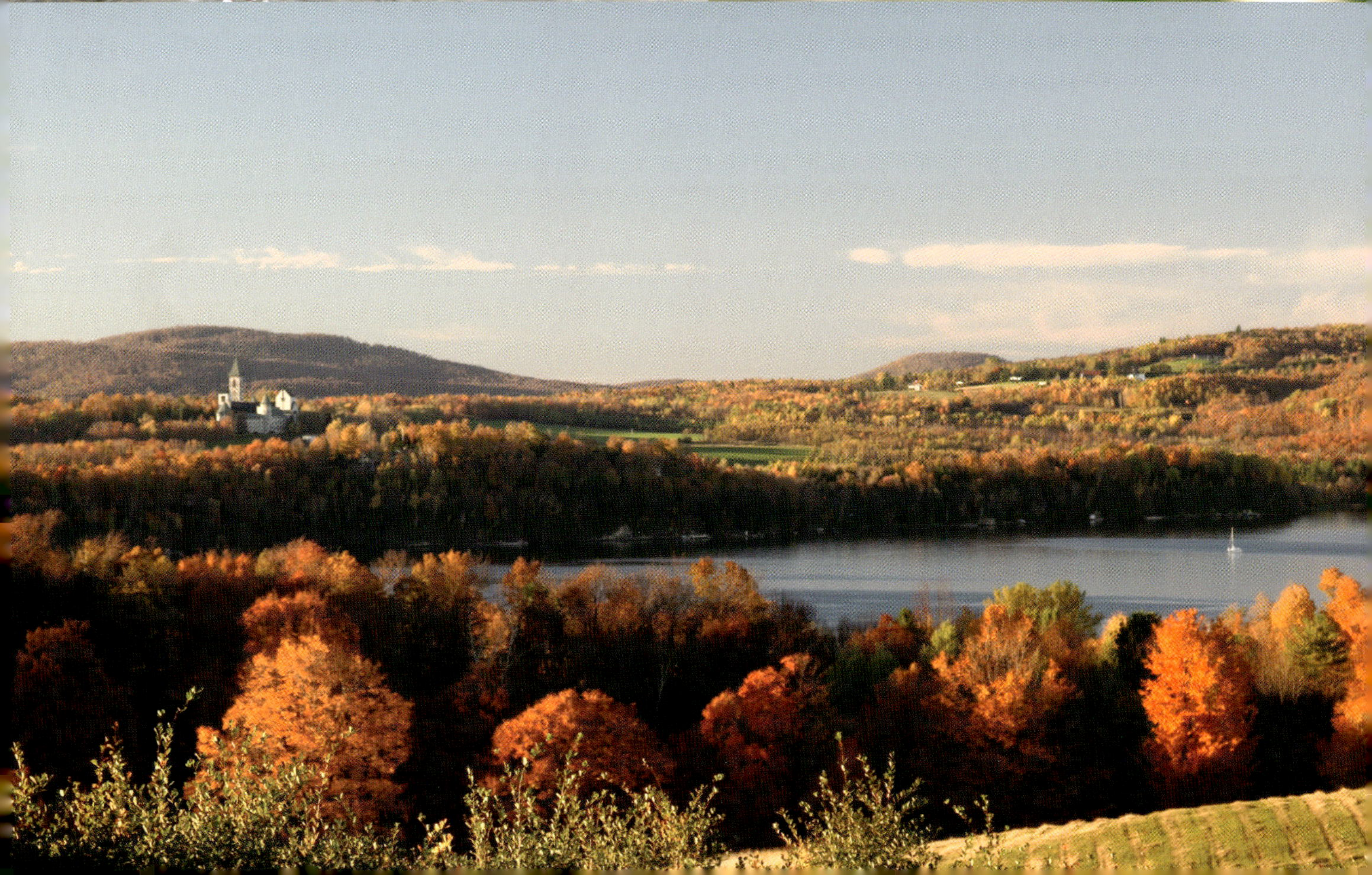

The Magnificent Eastern Townships

Driving along Autoroute 10 from Montreal or Autoroute 55 from Drummondville, you soon come to a superb region nestled between valleys and mountains, stretching from Granby to Lac-Mégantic and hugging 300 kilometres of American border. Its mountains (occupying 80% of the territory), lakes, and rivers are exquisite. Its people, who have always been attached to their history and traditions, are exceptional.

The religious heritage of the villages is apparent in their numerous churches. They are sometimes tiny, sometimes simple chapels of various denominations, built of wood and painted white. See them for example, in Bury, Georgeville, and Way's Mills, where they stand side by side or across from each other, greeting the parishioners together.

The countryside testifies to its agricultural heritage, telling its history through numerous covered bridges and round barns painted blood-red. These distinctive structures, which are not found in any similar number anywhere else in Quebec, were all built between 1901 and 1914. Many are still in excellent condition.

On a rural stretch of about 130 kilometres, mainly in the area of Cowansville, Dunham, East Stanbridge, and Saint-Armand, is the Wine Route. Here, wine growers tell visitors about the microclimate phenomenon and share the mysteries of wine growing and the art of winemaking. The route also features some exceptional apple groves that provide spectacular views during apple blossom season and real delights at picking time!

From the top of Cochrane road in Compton, the valley unfolds endlessly. Below, farming dominates a rich and colourful landscape in every season. Fresh farm products are for sale everywhere. Fields of sunflowers pleasantly surprise visitors around bends in the road, and in the heart of the countryside, cascading streams come crashing down, making sure no one forgets they are there.

On side roads in the Coaticook area, the lovely villages of Saint-Venant-de-Paquette and Saint-Herménégilde are visible from a distance. Much prettier than postcards!

Saint-Camille is a quiet and comforting refuge from a storm. It is one of the first villages to be established in the Eastern Townships, and a few of its original buildings are still standing, adding to its charm. Danville, for its part, bustles with the sophistication of a much larger place, as witnessed in its buzzing town square and the dynamism of its citizens.

Visitors have to drive through Milan and Nantes—the names conjuring up other countries—to reach the Lac-Mégantic region. Once here, there is much to appreciate, including the beauty of the lake, the pureness of the air, and the dazzling sunsets. There are also small communities encircling the lake, such as the village of Piopolis, that are worth a detour.

As you can see, there are a multitude of treasures to discover. All you need to do is visit—the magnificent Eastern Townships are waiting for you!

Flavours of a Region *Eastern Townships*

THE STORY OF THE LAND

The Eastern Townships harmoniously combines the wealth of Anglo-Saxon charm with a rich and resolutely Quebecois joie-de-vivre. The arrival of the American Loyalists and the English, Irish, and Scottish immigrants during the 18th and 19th centuries moulded a history that reveals itself around each bend in the road, be it in a small, quiet town or the luxuriant countryside.

The region was used by the Abenaki, members of the great Algonquin family, as a crossing zone and for hunting and trapping. The names of several villages, lakes, and rivers, including Coaticook, Massawippi, Memphremagog, Megantic, and Missisquoi, are from the Abenaki people.

It is a heavily forested region, populated by farmers and foresters. Large maple stands can frequently be seen at the edge of many of the farms here. Maple sap processing has long been a family activity in the Eastern Townships, so much so that some have deplored the failure to fully exploit the best maple products in Quebec. Nevertheless, maple products have significantly contributed to the growth of the region, just as the forests have generated wealth.

VALUES AND HERITAGE

The New England Loyalists shaped the face of the Eastern Townships. Between 1775 and 1810, thousands of farmers chose to settle in the Townships rather than in Upper Canada. Later on, immigrants from Ireland, Scotland, and other European countries, fleeing war or famine, came to settle here. Around 1850, the shortage of seigneurial lands in the St. Lawrence valley attracted French Canadians.

The region is rich with Loyalist tradition and architecture. An entirely French-speaking village often neighbours a primarily English-speaking one. Cohabitation has always been peaceful, and integration has occurred gradually and collaboratively. The residents of the Eastern Townships have never been at war with one another;

indeed, there is a certain homogeneity in the population, although no one attaches any great importance to it. They have preferred to build, rather than spend their time and energy quibbling. The strength of the communities lies in the choices they have made to integrate and find a happy medium, taking advantage of each other's knowledge and experience.

The gorgeous landscape unfolds in a wholesome environment and a climate favourable to farming. In addition, certain crops, such as the grape vine, are favoured by the microclimates that dot the territory. These optimal conditions for agricultural development are responsible for the undisputed high quality of the lovely dairy and beef cattle in the region and for the first-class produce grown here. The expertise and traditions of the English-speaking people have played a major role, and the positive integration of the peoples finds its natural reflection in the agriculture.

AGRICULTURE IN MODERN TIMES

Over time, agriculture diversified. It became industrialised but, unlike other regions, this development was never taken to unreasonable lengths. This is at least in part due to natural conditions that were not ideal for industrial farming techniques.

A wind of change blows in the Eastern Townships, as it does elsewhere in the province. Although it is the second most important lamb-breeding region in Quebec, younger people here are banking on diversity and breaking habits with respect to both breeding and production, creating new niches by raising duck, bison, deer, or wapiti.

Another refreshing change is the reappearance of time-honoured trades and practices. Many villages have traditional bakeries, and people head to the farm to buy milk, cream, or cheese, or visit the gardener for fruits and vegetables. There are also shepherds and goatherds working in the fields.

These artisans count on their superior breeding and production practices, which are part and parcel of the lifestyle they have chosen for themselves. Their values are solid and they seek contentment. They have chosen the Eastern Townships as their home, and they proudly offer their products at food fairs, in weekly baskets delivered to their clients, or in market stalls in Sherbrooke, Ayer's Cliff, North Hatley, Lac-Mégantic, and Danville. Their endeavours are the result of their questions and observations about the ability of people to rely on traditional practices in their daily lives.

The American, English, and French history in the Eastern Townships represents another wonderful opportunity for growth in culinary culture. Wine growers and chefs join with artisan producers to create dishes prepared with talent and originality. The region is also strategically located, with access to a population of approximately 2.5 million people, ensuring the influence of the people who live here.

Keepers of Time

Paul-André Blais was born in 1921, on Rang 10 in Saint-Camille, where his grandfather had settled after leaving Victoriaville in 1901. Paul-André and his wife Rollande Charland eventually bought farmland and settled down to raise a family.

"When I was young, I remember using a carriage to go places. In winter, we had to wait until the roads were packed down. They flattened snow with a big roller. Later, we used to go to church or the hospital by snowmobile. On Sundays, there would be heated discussions on the church steps. Everyone knew each other, and we talked about the sermon or politics."

At one time, most of the land in the area was wooded. Trees had to be cleared before it could be farmed. Stumps would eventually decay, but cumbersome rocks needed to be removed. "It took 'power' to do that. So we would harness our horses or yoke the oxen; we'd use chains for that. I worked with the oxen. At one time, the horses all got a disease. My uncle Émile had a pair of oxen, and so did other neighbours. My father really wanted some too. So we got some!

"There were two general stores in the village. Ah, competition! Even in those days…. We could find everything we needed, food, tools, nails, remnants. Women sewed and knitted with 'domestic' wool. In those days, there was a big demand for sheep's wool that was carded at the village mill."

Electricity arrived in 1946. The butcher would come to the farm to buy one animal, sometimes two, which he would then bring to Sherbrooke to sell at the public market on Fridays. At one time, there were as many as four butchers. Then the mobile abattoirs started appearing. For a two-hundred-pound pig, Paul-André Blais would receive three or four cents a pound. They had a modest income. "With six children to feed, we couldn't afford to fool around. Fortunately, we had everything we needed on the farm."

Waking up at four o'clock every morning to look after the animals, working in the fields, tapping maple trees in the spring to be sure there was enough syrup to last until the following spring, cooking on a wood stove, kneading bread, making preserves… if they had to do it over again, Rollande and Paul-André would not change a thing! They have lived their lives well and are proud to say so.

Lina Vaillancourt was born in Amqui in 1911. Only six months old when her father died, she had no way of knowing how it would drastically affect the course of her life. In 1914, her mother Herminie moved to Coaticook with her seven daughters, where she met Olivier Hébert and married him. They first settled on a small farm, and three years later purchased a larger one, with 25 dairy cows, lambs, chickens, turkeys, and pigs.

Lina, the youngest, was naturally resourceful and loved doing her chores on the farm. She knew how to do everything. She quit school at the age of 11. "We grew cereal grains, hay, and rutabagas to feed the cows. It's like a turnip that we would chop up and mix with the hay. It was their dessert!"

She then began her career as a milkwoman. She delivered milk to the neighbours, using a small pail. Later, she needed a horse and wagon to meet the growing demand for the natural milk. Customers would buy small quantities of milk, cream, and butter. It was so easy: milk cost six cents a quart and was delivered to the door, morning and evening.

"I was always on the road. I would harness up Catin, my beautiful mare, and off we would go with the wagon, after the animals were fed, the cows milked, and the milk bottled, of course. Catin would stop by herself at the doorstep to each house. I also ran errands. Among other things, I would pick up some elastic and braid at the Belding Corticelli factory and deliver them to women who would wrap them around small pieces of cardboard. I asked the priest for permission to wear pants, which was much more practical for jumping in and out of the cart. Soon other women started copying me!"

Lina would get up at four o'clock and "wrap elastic for Belding" until breakfast. "Not that it paid well, but it was a habit. Then the day's chores would begin with caring for the animals."

Her secret for a long life? "Work outdoors! If I wasn't outside, I was in the stable with the animals. I clipped cows, I washed them with laundry blue so their skin would be whiter, bled and plucked hens for Mr. Tremblay, looked after the neighbour's cows... it's incredible that I did all that! Thank God I was healthy!"

Lina and Arthur Roussel raised eight children, and they all delight in the rich history that Lina, age 96, so generously shares with them.

Flavours of a Region *Eastern Townships*

Charles-Henri de Coussergues
Vignoble de l'Orpailleur
Dunham

Charles-Henri de Coussergues was raised in the department of Gard, France, the son of a wine grower. After graduating in viticulture and oenology, he came to Quebec for a training program. "I saw the possibility of saving the wine-making culture. I just needed to find people who would believe in it enough to support me."

"Hervé Durand, a wine grower and my neighbour in France, wanted to invest in Quebec. We combined our know-how, we did a feasibility study—climate, temperature, rain, snow, dominant winds, ground composition, microclimates...."

The first vines, approximately 12,000 of them, were planted in Dunham in 1983, and the first bottles were produced in 1985. That is when the poet Gilles Vigneault christened the vineyard "l'Orpailleur" (the gold gatherer).

Pioneers in new areas of business cannot copy their neighbours or rely on existing documentation. "L'Orpailleur is an experimental farm. Some experiments went well, others didn't, and that is normal. The cultivation, the diseases, the production.... It's sad when you succeed agriculturally but then when you get to the press, nothing works.... There is no room in the world for average wines."

If he hadn't become a wine grower, Charles-Henri would have worked with wood as a cabinetmaker or cooper, two occupations he finds fascinating. Thanks to the complementary strengths of the team members and the enthusiasm of his partners Hervé Durand, Frank Furtado, and Pierre Rodrigue, it took 20 years to "make" l'Orpailleur. The success belongs to the team, and their numerous awards pay tribute to the efforts of all of them.

With 14 hectares of vines, it is the largest vineyard in Quebec. "We have six months to do what others do in a year. This limits large-scale development, but it is also what is charming about Quebec wines, which distinguish themselves through the specific characters of the many small businesses."

If not for the investment in regional development by the artisans of the Vignoble de l'Orpailleur, Quebec would probably not have the viticulture, wine making, and agrotourism that it does today.

See recipe page 92

Flavours of a Region *Eastern Townships*

HÉLÈNE DOUCET-LEVASSEUR
AU CŒUR DE LA POMME – *Frelighsburg*
FLEURS DE POMMIERS – *Dunham*

It started as a project to fill weekends and summer vacations. Originally from New Brunswick, Hélène and Steve Levasseur were business people who lived in Montreal and were looking for a country house. They wanted to breathe some fresh air, rest, enjoy fields and lakes, and go sailing.

They purchased a 135-acre apple orchard in Frelighsburg. "We had 5,000 dwarf apple trees in our backyard, and we didn't really know how they would perform. But then the little apples just showed up in June."

Apple growers despite themselves, the Levasseurs replaced the dwarf apple trees with other cultivars. Today, the orchard contains 6,000 apple trees of about ten varieties. "For ten years, we came on weekends. Then one day, we started making apple jelly and apple butter. We set up a picnic table, a stand…. We would start cooking at 6:00 a.m. on Saturday mornings, and by 9:00 a.m., the jars were on the shelves, still warm."

Today, au Cœur de la pomme is an artisan vinegar factory that produces exceptional apple cider vinegars. The traditional process guarantees an entirely natural product, and the vinegar is aged for one year in oak barrels and is not filtered or pasteurized. Their daughter Stéphanie, "who would never go back to live in town", is very involved, and will eventually take over and ensure the continuity of the family business.

In 1989, the Levasseurs purchased a 70-acre apple orchard on the Wine Route in Dunham, with 10,000 dwarf, semi-dwarf, and standard apple trees, and plunged into the world of cider making. In 2004, they introduced a "fire cider" to complete the family of cider products offered here. Unlike the process used to make ice cider, the juice of apples is heated in a sugar shack, infusing the cider with maple and walnut flavours.

See page 27

Annick Savaria
Menthe Fraîcheur
Coaticook

On the mountainside near her home, Annick Savaria grows mint. Among the varieties are spearmint and peppermint, along with specialty flavours like ginger, grapefruit, green apple, and pineapple mint.

"I spent a lot of time at my grandmother's bedside, and I remember that she would often get little soaps as gifts. They were made with vegetables and plants, like carrot and mint, and I was fascinated by them. I loved the smell of mint, not to mention its health benefits. One day, I discovered mint growing at the foot of a big fir tree. I forgot that I had planted a mint and green apple hybrid plant."

Sparked by this discovery, Annick immediately thought of growing mint on a large scale and processing it. Her research was fruitful and her tests with various cultivars—a full range of flavours—were conclusive. First, she turned the mint into cooking products, but she soon began to create other products, ones that also nourish the body, but through the pores of the skin.

Today, Menthe Fraîcheur, Atmosphère & Spa is housed in the old Coaticook railway station. This building features the largest train station rotunda in Quebec, and is a wonderful retreat steeped in cultural heritage and suffused with peace and harmony. She has recently joined forces with a renowned skin care product manufacturer and now offers a complete range of plant-based skin care products, made with the mint that grows in her garden.

"A spa where the mint I grow would be used? This is a project that I dreamed of, but I thought it would come true much later in life. However, circumstances were such that I plunged in, body and soul, much sooner than I anticipated."

Menthe Fraîcheur, Atmosphère & Spa offers special gourmet treats for the body.

See page 125

Diane Beaulieu and Jean-Noël Groleau
Beurrerie du Patrimoine
Compton

Diane Beaulieu is categorical: she will not compromise on the quality of her products. Health comes first, then her personal taste: "If I wouldn't eat it, it's not for sale."

"We were five children at home, but my mother would take care of neighbourhood children, sometimes for a long time. Including my parents, there were easily 25 mouths to feed. I soon learned to cook, using the best products available on the farm."

After Diane got married and settled in Compton, she was pained to see that people here did not have the opportunity to try the high quality milk and maple products that she was used to. They started with maple products and soon Jean-Noël Groleau farm products were available in agricultural fairs and food shows all over the province.

Once their three boys became teenagers, they told their parents that they wanted to work with them on the farm. But 50 cows were not enough! They would need to purchase a larger milk quota, as well as more land and farm buildings, representing an enormous investment that would take years to become profitable.

Diane and Jean-Noël therefore decided to process on the premises. This way, the whole family could work together, distributing the tasks among themselves. They made cheese and yogurt and bottled milk and cream. In 2004, they reached back into the past and began making traditional butter with fresh cream.

Alex, Patrick, and Sylvain are the fifth generation of Groleau farmers. They have Holstein dairy cows, as well as Canadian cows, the oldest North American cattle race. On the top floor of the barn there is a dairy cow interpretation centre, an excellent way for visitors to enrich their knowledge.

See recipe page 100

Martine Paridaens and Normand Vigneau
Les jardins du ruisseau Ball
Way's Mills

Martine Paridaens came from Belgium in 1978 and settled with her brother on a farm in Barnston, near Coaticook. Normand Vigneau, originally from the Magdalen Islands, travelled through France before coming here to look for work. That was when he met Martine.

For ten years, they lived in Montreal. Martine taught fabric printing and Normand taught French. They came back here every weekend and eventually started looking for a farm where they could live permanently.

The artisan gardeners first launched a medicinal plant cultivating project, but the end result failed to meet their expectations. They wanted to stand out from the crowd, and they were drawn to old and forgotten vegetable varieties.

They moved to Way's Mills, and by 2000, their vegetables were at the Ayer's Cliff and North Hatley farmers markets.

They grow a fascinating variety of vegetables, including pink and rocambole garlic, twenty kinds of potatoes and tomatoes, ten types of cucumber, purple snow peas, fifteen sorts of lettuce, squash, artichokes, Jerusalem artichokes, white and rattail radishes, to name but a few.

The "Visitors' Garden" is the most interesting area of the farm, featuring over 200 varieties of vegetables, not to mention herbs and berries. Higher up, on the plateau, is the market garden.

"Our 'Visitors' Garden' lets people see vegetables in their different stages of growth. This is the educational aspect that we wanted to develop. You find about three plants of each variety growing. We are thrilled when our 'Discovery' or 'Sample' baskets, which we deliver to our clients every week or sell at the market, manage to stir up our customers' curiosity and brighten their day. Some children come back to buy the white or the lemon cucumber they liked, sometimes with their own pocket money. This encourages us to push our research further."

See page 30

Carole Huppé and Richard Côté
Miellerie Lune de miel
Stoke

Richard had dreamed of being a beekeeper for a long time. He finally purchased about ten hives, which he installed on his father's farmland. Nearby was a deserted motel cabin with love messages written on the walls, and this is where he got the inspiration to name his bee farm "Lune de miel" (Honeymoon).

He and Carole settled in Stoke in 1982. Their goal was not only to keep bees and process honey, but to create an educational wing and interest visitors of all ages in the amazing world of bees.

They welcomed groups to their modest building, and gave them information along with samples of the delicious, pure honey. Total annual production is approximately 20,000 kilograms, the yield varying with the weather and the season. The hives are strategically placed in different areas and produce blueberry, apple, raspberry, and clover honey.

The couple were encouraged by the public's interest, and the bee farm grew. They added new products. While Richard was smitten with beekeeping, Carole was entranced by their cleverness, by the operation of the hive as a well-organized society, and by the fragility of our environment. This inspired her idea of a giant beehive, which has since been installed. Walking through it is like a visit to a real-life fairy tale setting!

"I'm hooked on research. I can never know enough. I'm interested in the latest scientific discoveries. If only I could read their minds, discover their way of seeing objects, know more about the benefits of a sting from these 'winged pharmacists'. There are still so many discoveries to be made. Did you know that if bees disappeared from the earth, we would lose 30% of the food we presently consume?

"We loved bees, but we didn't even know how much. Of course, there have been sacrifices, but they are worth it. We think our bees are beautiful—they are like our children!"

See page 33

PIERRE-YVES CLERSON
LES BONTÉS DIVINES
Stoke

Pierre-Yves Clerson worked as a graphic artist for 15 years. As the artistic director of a well-known Sherbrooke area communications firm, he certainly did not suspect that one day he would be breeding web-footed birds!

"It was during a trip to France, in the Gers region in particular, where I have family, that I discovered duck products. I was so completely captivated by this type of breeding that I actually decided to abandon my career for it. I remember that it was so unusual, so unknown, I felt like I was jumping off a cliff."

He and his wife Catherine spent three years looking for the ideal farm. They had determined the ingredients that were essential for a good quality of life. They wanted to stay in the region but in a rural area, although not too far from schools and services for Frédérick, Pierre-Olivier, and Maxence, who were growing up fast. They also needed an old house with a well-kept barn.

Pierre-Yves, the artisan producer, returned to the Gers to learn his trade. "At first, I didn't even know how many birds I should buy or what to feed them. I was also totally useless at gavage techniques!"

Today, Barbarie ducks are 12 weeks old when they reach the Bontés Divines farm. Raised without antibiotics or animal fat, once they reach the desired weight, they are gently force-fed round corn kernels by hand, twice a day for three weeks.

In addition to the 500 male Barbarie ducks, there are about one hundred chickens that are ready after about 90 days, and for fun, a couple of wild turkeys, a few hunting ducks, three goats, and two rabbits.... A great farm visit!

The duck products sold here are processed by hand using traditional European techniques. Choose from a dizzying array, including foie gras mi-cuit, confits, magrets, mousses, terrines, dry sausages, and more. A gift from heaven!

See recipes pages 66, 68 and 80

Flavours of a Region *Eastern Townships*

Mariandrée Dubois
Florasel
Saint-Camille

Born in Montreal from a French father and a Haitian mother, Mariandrée Dubois studied management and horticulture, despite her marked talents in the fine arts.

Entirely self-taught, Mariandrée expressed her gifts through painting. She never wanted to create paintings to hang on museum walls—she preferred the living arts and her own unique signature. She was also a sculptor, sometimes using recycled plastics or fabrics. Creation was her raison d'être.

Then, about fifteen years ago, at a clothes exhibit at the Centre communautaire and culturel du P'tit Bonheur, Mariandrée fell under the spell of the village of Saint-Camille.

She then felt the urge to create something else. Her studies in horticulture brought her closer to the earth. "It gave me an opportunity to commune with nature. Edible flowers are important to me again, because I know that I have always been drawn to medicinal plants, although I was not necessarily looking to promote them. Today I want to share the joy of gardening, the pleasures of tasting, of doing something that associates the useful with the practical and brings healthy pleasure. When we play with flowers, we are on another plane, in another dimension. We are attuned to the life force, and we see things more closely."

She has also written a book, dedicated to edible flowers. Mariandrée felt a creative urge to express herself through food and has turned to creating flower sea salts. "Salt is magic; it lets me play with colour. Salt totally envelops and captures the exact colour of the petals and awakens subtle flavours." For a painter and colourist, flower sea salts made with daylilies, marigolds, gladioli are magic, or the closest thing to it.

See page 123

Julie Roy and Jacky Traver
Domaine des Travers du Roy
Stratford

Jacky worked as a shepherd for six years when he was still in France, where the trade is taught in agricultural training colleges specializing in sheep breeding.

One day he came to Quebec with a friend, and they never went back. For 12 years, they operated a dairy farm and in 1992, they sold their milk quota. Jacky naturally fell into raising slaughter lambs.

Once the first dairy ewes had been brought to Canada (by a Quebecer, as it happens), it was easy for Jacky to transform his herd and begin producing sheep's milk. In 1999, Julie and Jacky settled on a small, unworked farm in the Lac-Mégantic area. They built a dairy and a milking room and created two sheep-pens.

In 2004, Julie and Jacky set up a dairy ewe interpretation centre to inform the public about these adorable creatures. The video tells us everything about their lives: milking, the benefits of the milk, the uses of wool, and so on. This is followed by a visit to the farm and milking room and finally, a cheese tasting. Other sheep products, such as soap, wool, and meat, can also be purchased on the premises.

Julie and Jacky's mission is to produce high-quality milk, and they work hard to ensure that it happens. They also transport their exceptional milk to a specialised artisan cheese-making facility, where it is transformed into a unique cheese. This rare treat is available on the premises.

There is much to see here: the sheep grazing in the fields and, in particular, the ewe-lambs in their enclosure. These delightful creatures are tame, sweet, curious, and oh-so adorable.

See page 33

Flavours of a Region *Eastern Townships*

ISABELLE COUTURIER
CHÈVRERIE FRUIT D'UNE PASSION
Saint-Ludger

"This is where I will spend the rest of my days!" affirms Isabelle. "Only one month after moving here, I felt a deep attachment to this land." The dream began in Sainte-Marguerite, in the Beauce, but the search for a farm brought Isabelle Couturier and Alain Larochelle to Saint-Ludger in December 2004.

Born near Quebec City, in a rural area that was not agricultural at all, she never thought that she would end up living on a farm. "One day, we stopped at a farm where they were raising three or four goats. The farmer poured some goat milk in the coffee he gave us, and we were smitten!"

Isabelle studied geography, but found that it was not her calling. Instead, she decided to plant trees for reforestation, and then turned to farming. She enjoys manual work and, most of all, she loves being in nature. Alain, for his part, is trained as a computer scientist. Quite a world away from a farm!

They preferred to start with a smaller production volume and began with 20 goats. Today they own about one hundred, and they both work at it full time, enjoying a variety of tasks and taking turns with cheese-making and caring for the goats.

The Tomme des Joyeux Fromagers cheese was created for cheese lovers. In June 2006, Isabelle received a Caseus award for the best goat cheese in its category—just recognition for the work of a pioneer.

Isabelle is the kind of person who really sinks her teeth into life. If she had to do it over again, she would follow the same path. "In five years, in ten years, I picture myself here on the farm, running back and forth between the goats and cheese-making, marvelling at a newborn's pink nose…. I see myself answering the telephone and speaking to a chef who has just discovered our cheese and wants to use it in his recipes."

See recipes pages 72, 82 and 86

Aline Crête
Création Aline Crête
Magog

My eyes cannot decide where to rest, and they flit from one of the many fine porcelain objects in this room to another. I cannot wait to see them up close. Suddenly, there is only the woman, the artist Aline Crête, and her conversation in the bright workshop.

"If I had been more sensible, I would have gone into medicine. That would have been thinking with my head. My heart, however, was much happier being creative." So she listened to her heart.

Aline studied fine arts in Montreal. She converted a room into a modest workshop, taught ceramics and plastic arts, made art objects, exhibited at the Montreal Salon des métiers d'art, and raised two children.

While travelling in France in the late 1990s, she became inspired by Limoges porcelain. The idea of painting on fine porcelain appealed to her, and after much research, she found a painter from Limoges who agreed to teach her how. She studied in the workshop at the Musée Adrien-Dubouché, "the" Limoges porcelain museum.

"Mme Rahil taught me everything I could have hoped for, times a hundred. And with history lessons, too! Just finding myself in the gardens of the museum was already much more that I had ever dreamed of."

Aline mainly paints on practical objects. She finds inspiration in her garden. "Any subject is good. This trade lets me do what I like best: some graphic art, some calligraphy, some drawing...." Painting on porcelain requires precision, rigour, and patience, in addition to sensitivity and sophistication.

"I plunged in, with my heart and my soul. Of course, you have to keep a cool head to maintain a certain balance. I think it was my way of finding my own identity and exceeding my own limits, of going beyond what is known, beyond appearances."

See page 123

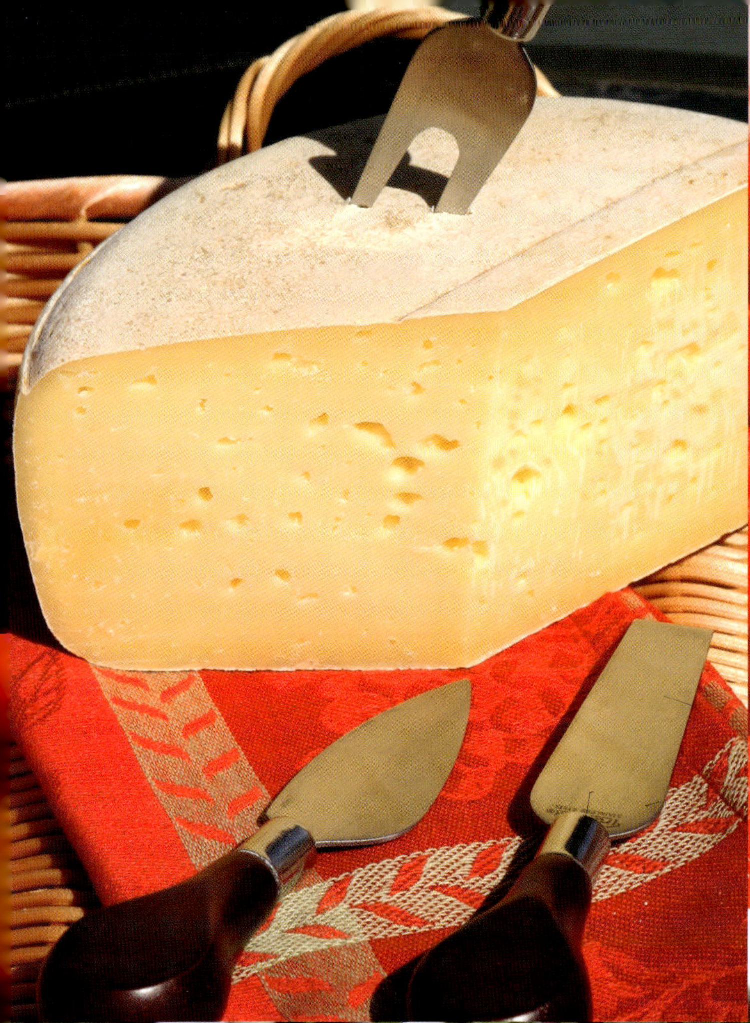
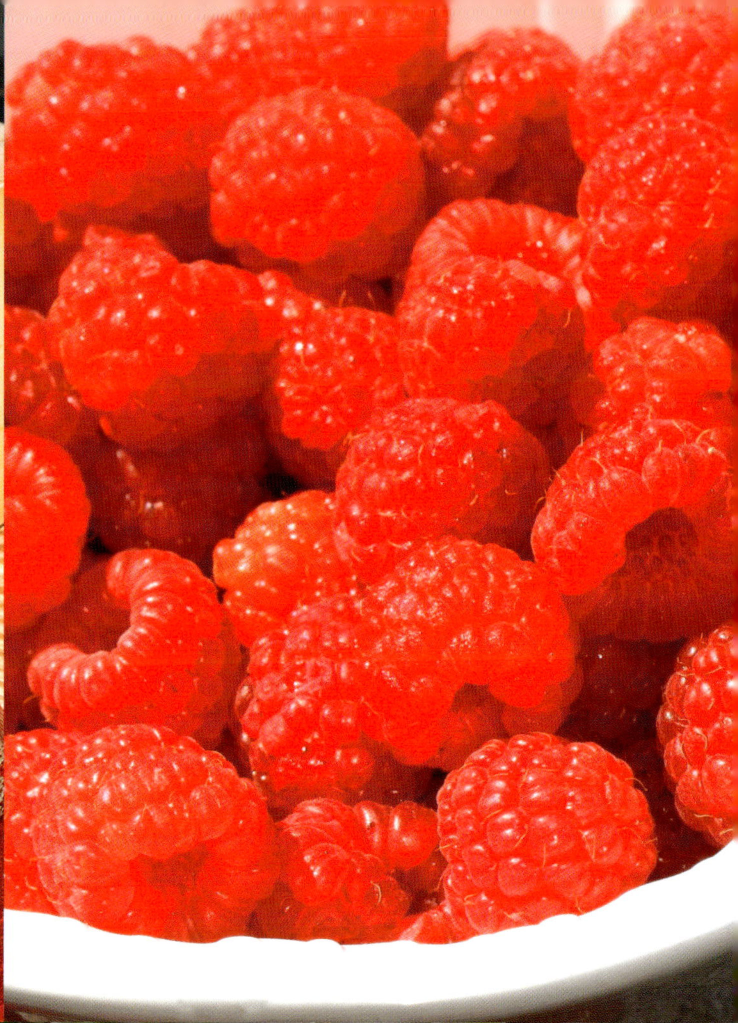
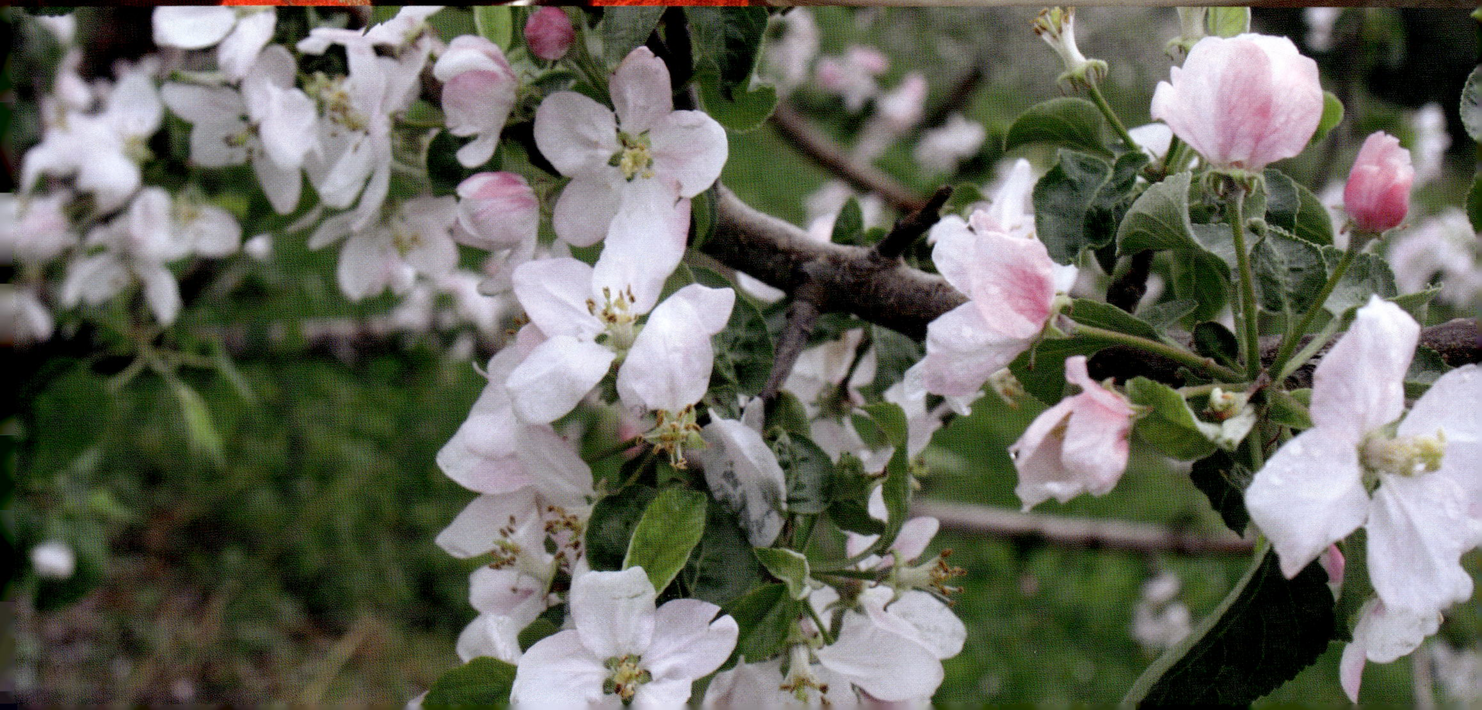

Flavours of a Region *Eastern Townships*

Backroad Treasures

Some good addresses for serious foodies!

BROME-MISSISQUOI

Hughes Ouellet is a happy artisan, a cheese maker with extensive experience, and now a specialist in the creation of raw milk cheeses. The distinctive aroma and flavour of his cheeses derive from the milk of Jersey cows, which are quite rare in Quebec.

Zéphir is a firm, washed-rind cheese with a very pleasant bouquet, recalling the mild breeze ("zephyr") that inspired its name. His second cheese, Brise du vigneron, is a soft cheese with a rustic rind. Fragrant and well-balanced, it will charm the most discriminating palate.

FROMAGERIE DES CANTONS

441 boul. De Normandie N., Farnham   450-293-2498   *see recipe page 50*

The vine and wine Economuseum® tells the story of the origins of viticulture and wine-making, and houses objects used in traditional practices, such as a wooden press, demijohns, billhooks, hoes, and artefacts from the 17th to the 20th centuries. A history lesson and a guided tour of the vineyards are nicely capped off with a tasting of their most successful creations.

VIGNOBLE DE L'ORPAILLEUR AND THE VINE AND WINE ECONOMUSEUM®

1086 Route 202, Dunham   450-295-2763   www.orpailleur.ca   *see page 15*

There are ice ciders, and then there is the Pommeau d'or, which has been dubbed a "fire cider" because it is created by evaporating the juice of apples over wood-fired heat. Definitely a comforting drink to curl up with. These artisans also are master vinegar makers and offer an impressive range of products of outstanding quality.

CIDRERIE FLEURS DE POMMIERS

1047 Route 202, Dunham   450-295-2223   www.fleursdepommiers.ca

and

AU CŒUR DE LA POMME

42 Route 237 N., Frelighsburg   450-298-5319   *see page 16*

At the foot of Mount Pinnacle, Sylvie Campbell, her husband François, and their children Mathieu, Keven, and Kim run a farm specializing in Mulard duck breeding. They offer visitors a vast array of duck products prepared on the premises, as well as other meats such as lamb, rabbit, goose, and guinea-fowl, also raised on the farm. A visit here is an excellent opportunity to take in the beautiful scenery, ramble through the apple orchard and on the forest paths, and enjoy a picnic on the grass.

LA GIRONDINE

104 Route 237 S., Frelighsburg   450-298-5206   www.lagirondine.ca

May is apple blossom season, a perfect time for a detour to Domaine Pinnacle, where you can enjoy a breathtaking view over a valley stretching to the mountains across the border in the United States. It is also a perfect opportunity to try appetizing and creative beverages, such as the award-winning Pinnacle ice cider or its sparkling cousin. Enhance the experience!

DOMAINE PINNACLE
150 Chemin Richford, Frelighsburg 450-298-1222 www.icecider.com

Although Brome Lake Ducks was founded in 1912 and is the oldest Peking duck farm in Canada, it uses only the latest and most advanced breeding techniques and feeding methods. The store offers a wide variety of fresh, frozen, or canned products, in various sizes. Plenty of delicacies to take home.

BROME LAKE DUCKS
40 Chemin du Centre, Knowlton 450-242-3825
www.canardsdulacbrome.com *see recipe page 68*

MEMPHREMAGOG

A visit to the interpretation centre and the sheepfold is a chance for young and old alike to learn all about sheep and sheep raising. The Balayer family also has a donkey farm, which gives visitors the opportunity to rediscover these charming, misunderstood, and largely forgotten creatures, who have sadly disappeared from rural life.

FERME LE SEIGNEUR DES AGNEAUX ET ASINERIE DU ROHAN
262 Chemin de la Diligence, Stukely-Sud 450-297-2662 or 1-866-330-2662
www.leseigneurdesagneaux.com

On top of Applegrove Hill are blue fields of lavender. Yes, lavender! The warm, dry climate and the 300-metre altitude provide good growing conditions, but the real credit has to go to Pierre Pellerin who, with much determination and patience, has established the first lavender farm in Quebec.

A visit here, even for just a few hours, is like stepping into a different world. See, touch, smell, and even taste the lavender grown here, for an incomparable sensory experience. Visit the interpretation centre for information about essential oil extraction methods before taking a walk through the fields—and don't forget your camera! The store offers several lavender-based products, including herbs, candies, jellies, and tea.

BLEU LAVANDE
891 Chemin Narrow, Fitch Bay 819-876-5851
www.bleulavande.ca *see recipes pages 62 and 100*

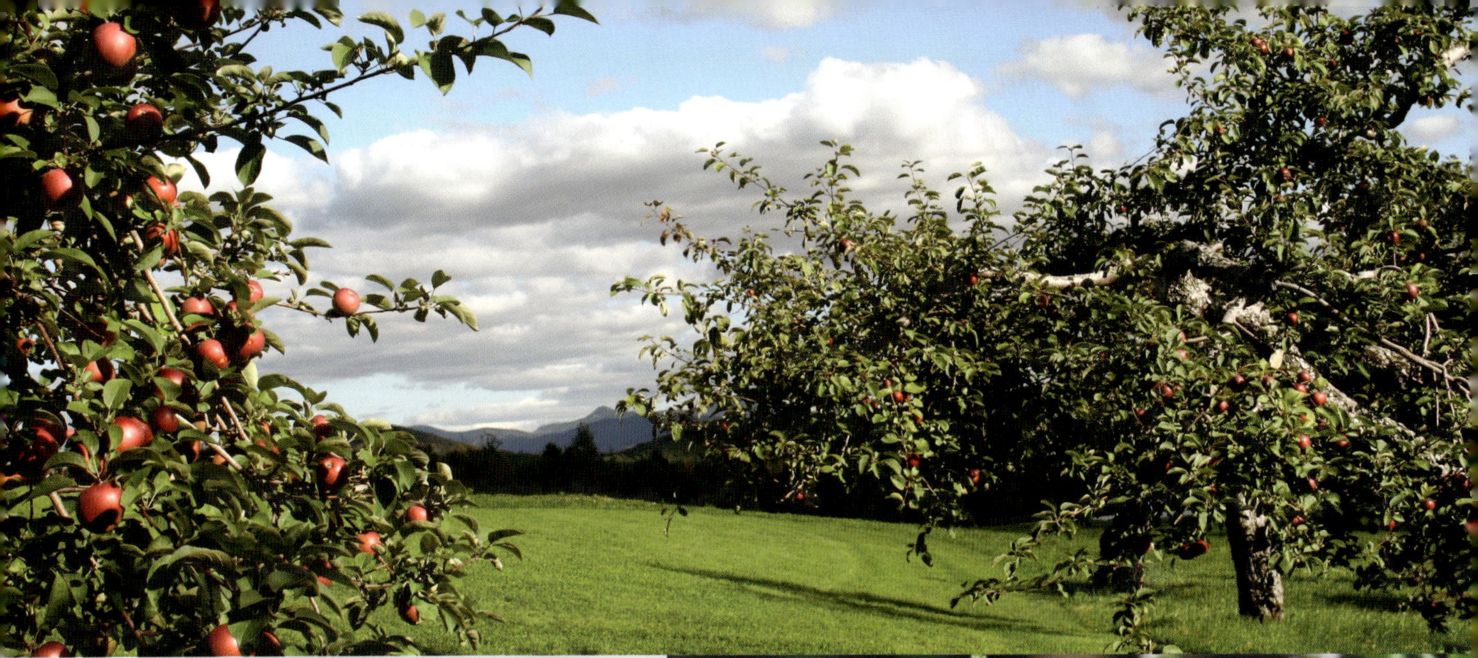

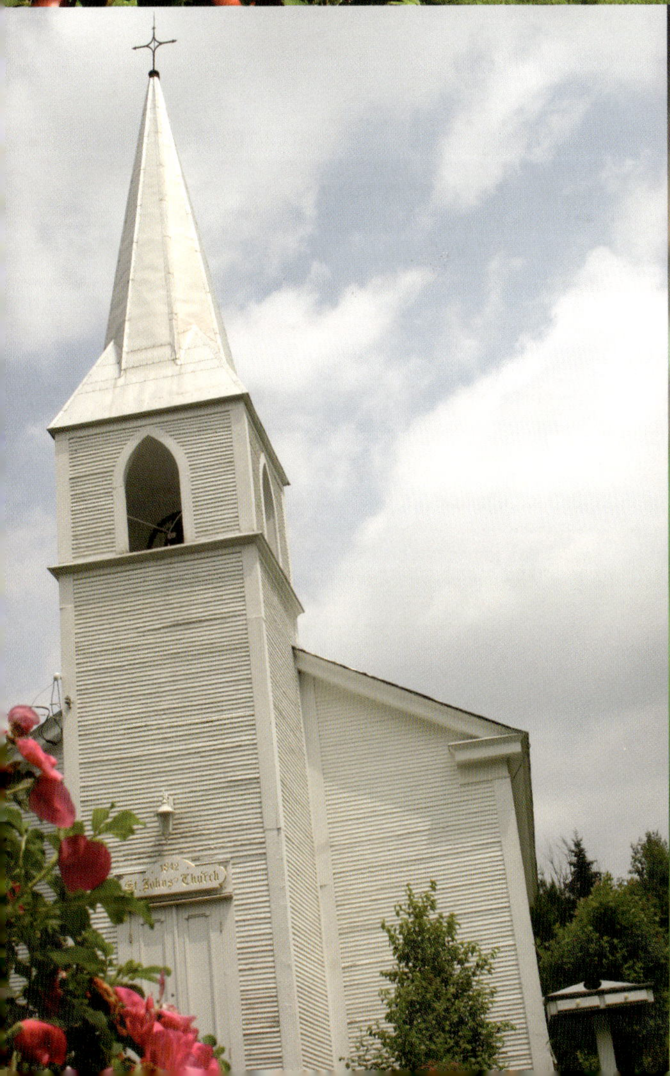
St. Johns Church

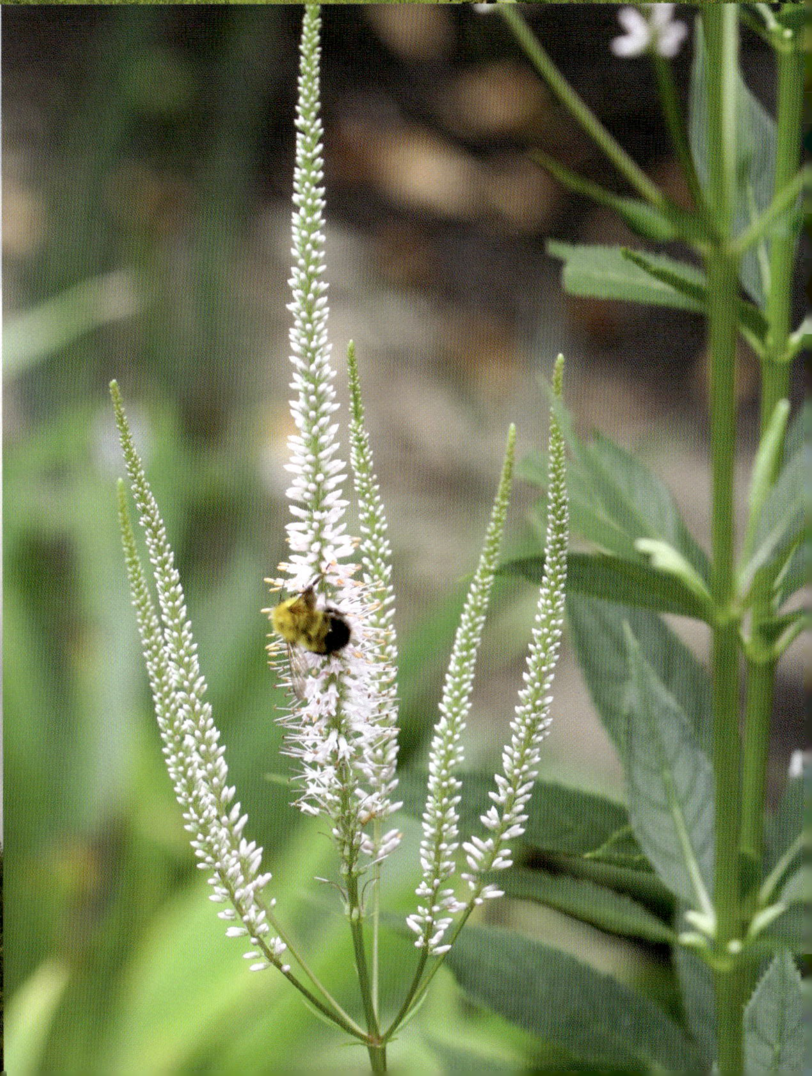

COATICOOK

The blackcurrants grown in the fields and the wild blackberries picked from the banks of Moe's River in Compton are the basic ingredients for two very pleasant and high-quality aperitif wines. Visitors here will learn about fruit wine-making and taste the slightly sweet wines. They can also stock up on Apéritif de cassis and Murmures, as well as syrups, vinegars, mustards, jellies, and preserves, to name but a few of the delicious products available.

APÉRI-FRUITS COMPTON 819-837-0301 or 1-877-737-0301
12 Chemin Boyce, Compton   www.produitsdelaferme.com/aperi-fruits

Hatley road is the kind of country road I like, running like a ribbon through the beautiful rural setting of Compton. Suddenly the Fromagerie La Station appears, where Carole Routhier greets her visitors with her biggest smile and speaks with pride of "the fruit of four generations of passionate work." Her son, cheese-maker Simon-Pierre Bolduc, produces raw milk farmstead cheeses, as tasty as they are fragrant.

The Comtomme is a semi-hard cheese, while Alfred le fermier is a hard cheese, aged at least 6 months. Every week features a different "special edition" cheese that has undergone a secret aging process for over 18 months. The products of this delicious secret are sold exclusively at the farm's cheese shop.

FROMAGERIE LA STATION 819-835-5301
440 Chemin Hatley, Compton   www.fromagerielastation.com   *see recipe page 78*

In the "Visitors' Garden", discover over 200 varieties of vegetables, herbs, and berries, and study them in their various stages of growth. Marvel at the pink or rocambole garlic, twenty kinds of potatoes and tomatoes, ten types of cucumber, purple snow peas, fifteen sorts of lettuce, squash, artichoke….

LES JARDINS DU RUISSEAU BALL
Way's Mills   819-876-2210   *see page 19*

One building houses an interpretation centre (where you can find out everything you ever wanted to know about the dairy cow) and another, a butter making facility and a butter museum. It is also a place to meet the producers, chat with them, and learn about their daily activities. At the store, stock your icebox with farmer's cream, cheeses, yogurt, butter, and other delicious dairy products.

BEURRERIE DU PATRIMOINE
225 Chemin Cochrane, Compton   819-835-9373   www.fermegroleau.com   *see page 18*

Founded in 1940, this family business is famous for its old-fashioned ice cream. It is the largest ice cream manufacturer in Quebec, and the ice cream is still made according to the original recipe. It contains no modified milk products and most of the flavourings used are natural.

The tasty challenge awaiting visitors is the array of flavours to choose from. Will it be blueberry, strawberry, or raspberry? Or will you sample the maple taffy ice cream, sold exclusively at the ice cream counter?

LAITERIE DE COATICOOK
1000 rue Child, Coaticook   819-849-2272 ou 1-800-846-7224
   www.laiteriedecoaticook.com   *see recipe page 102*

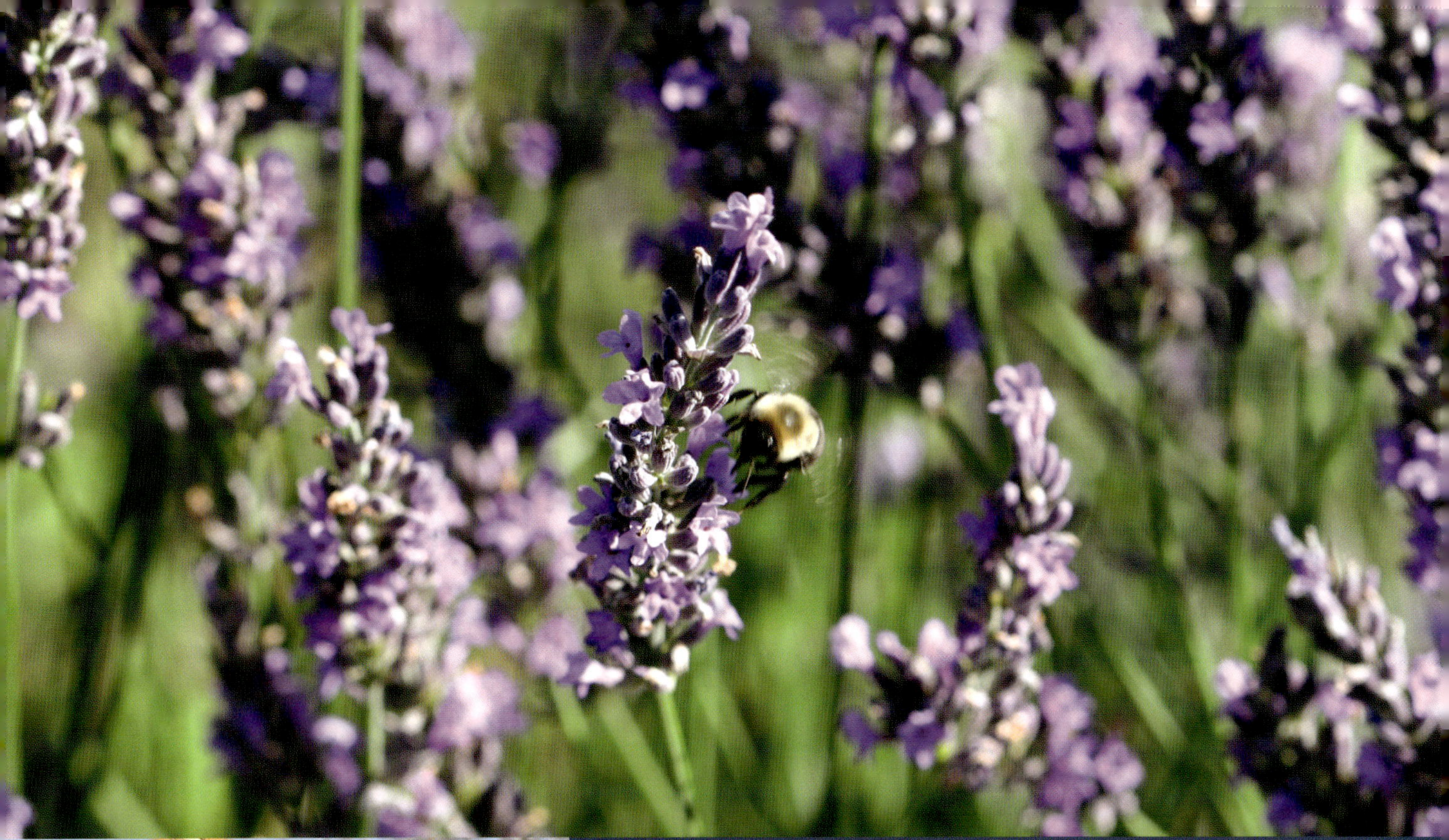

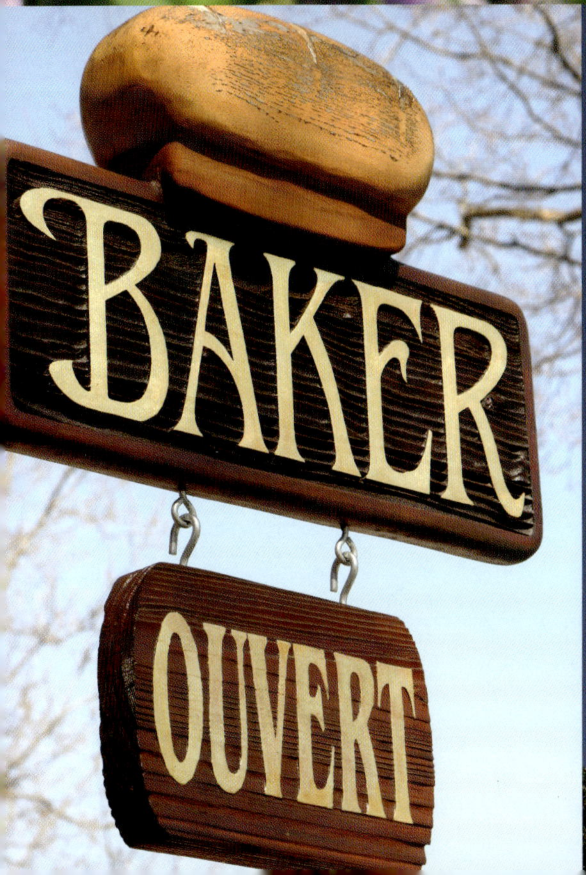
BAKER
OUVERT

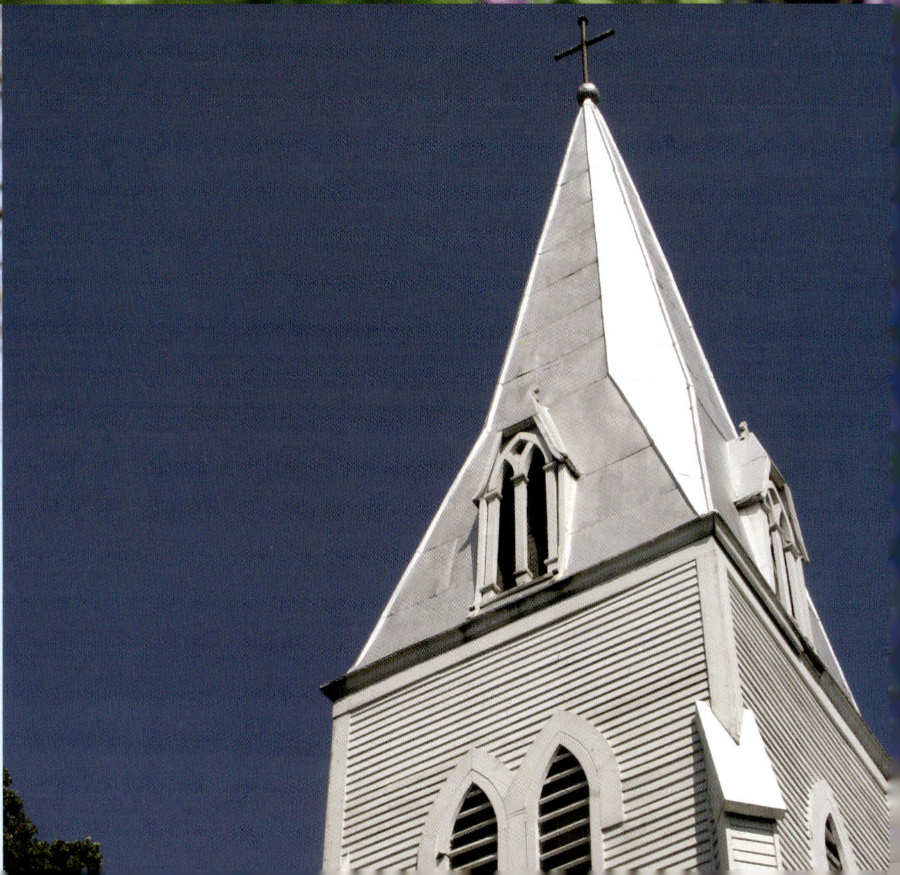

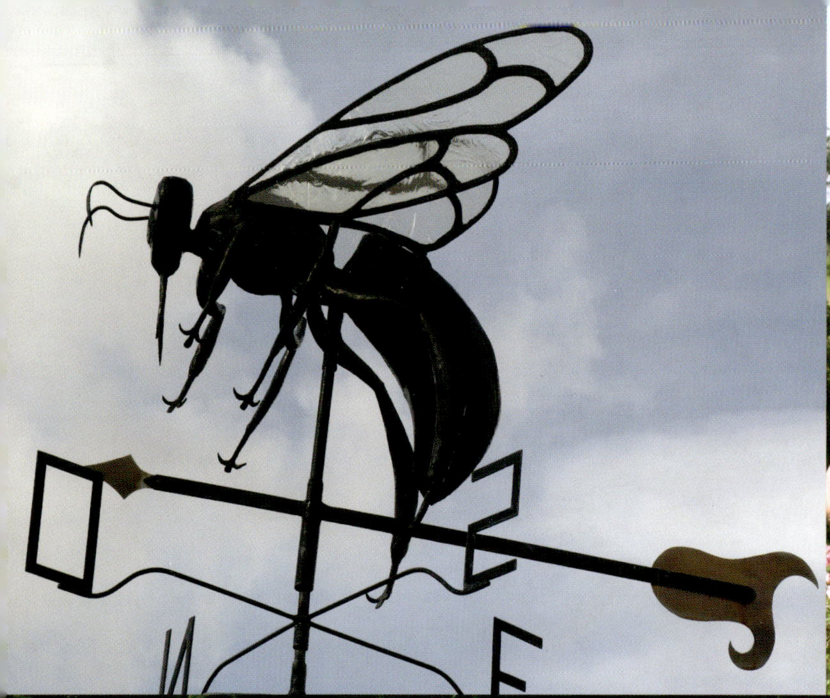

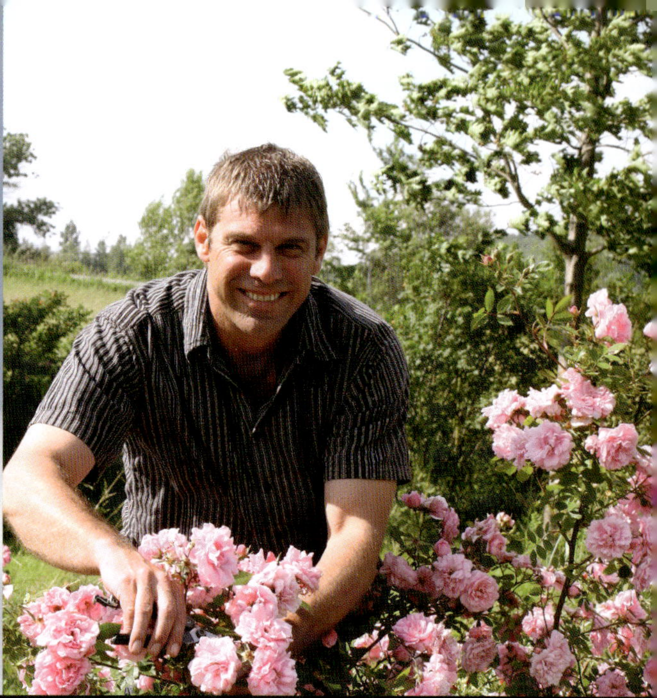

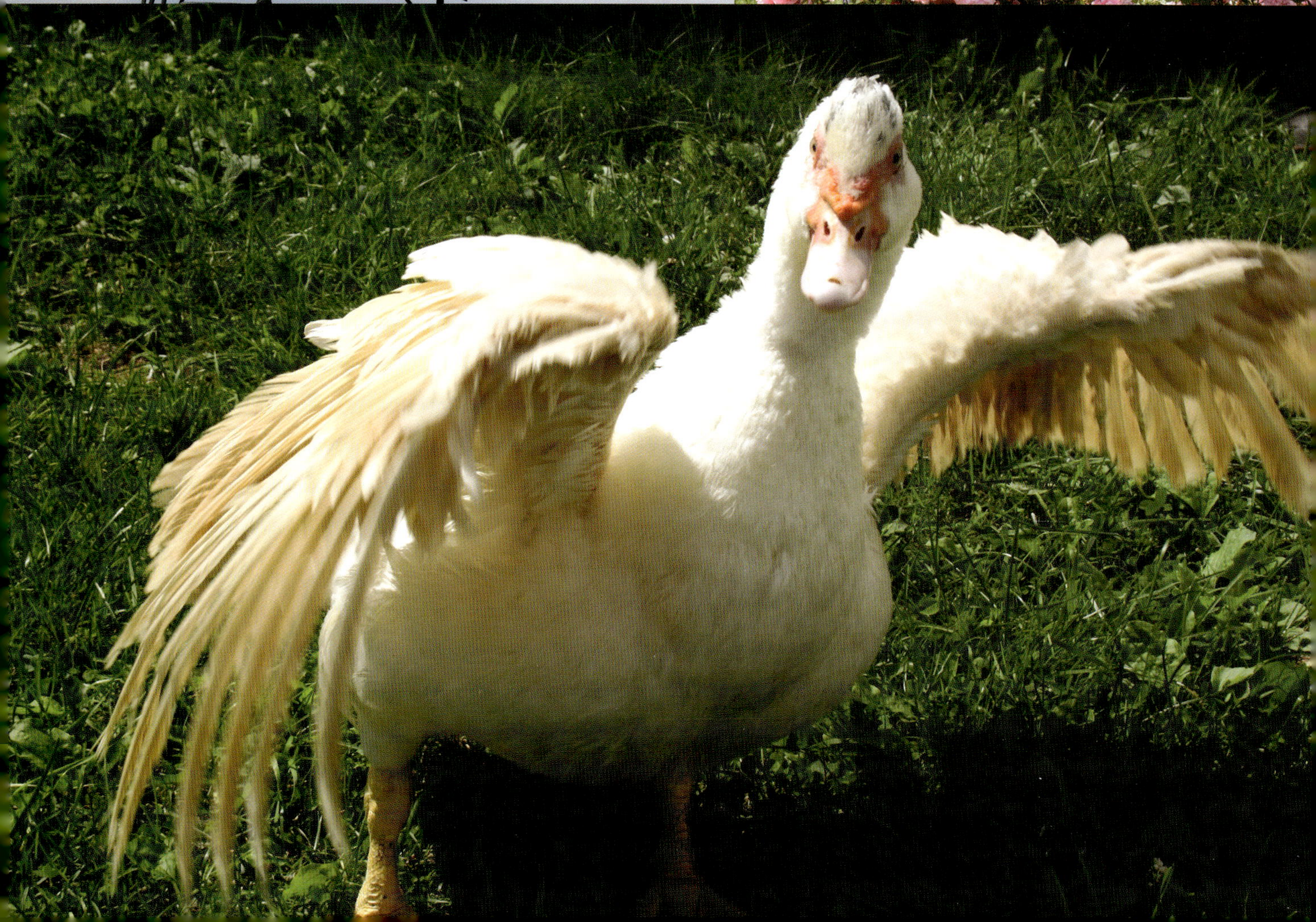

In a century-old maple stand, the Martineaus are busy greeting visitors. The family still carries on its original business of serving meals and turning maple sap into syrup, sugar, and caramel, always ensuring that the highest quality standards are maintained.

In the spring, also known as sugaring off season, meals are served in the sugar shack with all the traditional trappings. In the summer, visitors can spend time at the farm, feed the animals, have a picnic, and see the apple orchard and the vegetable garden. Delicious maple products are available at the boutique all year long.

FERME MARTINETTE
1728 Chemin Martineau, Coaticook   819-849-7089 or 1-888-881-4561
                                          www.lafermemartinette.com

HAUT-SAINT-FRANÇOIS

Did you know that if bees disappeared from the earth, we would lose 30% of the food we presently consume? Learn all about this well-organized society and walk through a giant beehive. A real-life fairy tale!

MIELLERIE LUNE DE MIEL
252 Rang 3 Est, Stoke   819-346-2558
                               www.miellerielunedemiel.com   *see page 20*

Visit the farm to learn about Barbarie duck breeding and see chickens, wild turkeys, hunting ducks, goats, and rabbits. The duck products on sale at the farm are processed by hand using traditional European methods.

LES BONTÉS DIVINES
255 Chemin Carrier, Stoke   819-878-3035
                                   www.divinesbontes.com   *see page 21*

Bruno Girard has been growing organic roses at the foot of Beauvoir Sanctuary for a few years now. His magnificent flowers are used in the small-scale manufacturing of jellies, rose-petal honey, vinegar, and other, wholly natural products. An original way to give your loved one – or yourself – some roses.

LA ROSE DE NEL
Stoke   819-562-2440

GRANIT

The Domaine des Travers du Roy features an interpretation centre about the dairy ewe, with a video on the day-to-day lives of the animals and then a visit to the farm and the milking room. A cheese tasting follows. Don't miss the ewe-lambs in their enclosure. These delightful creatures are tame, sweet, curious, and very, very adorable.

DOMAINE DES TRAVERS DU ROY
485 avenue Centrale S., Stratford   418-443-2020   www.traversduroy.com   *see page 23*

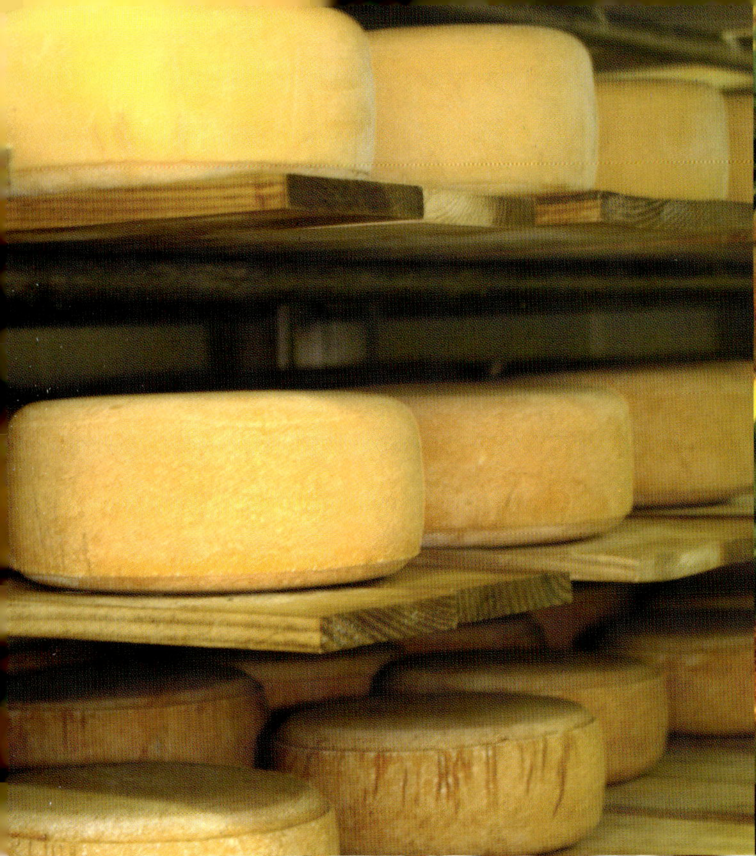
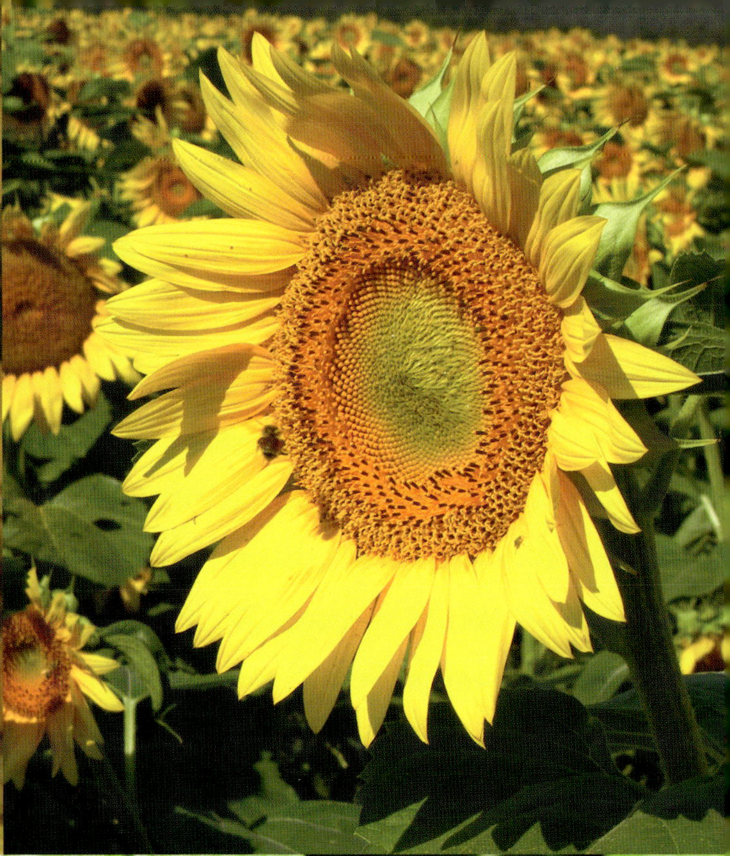
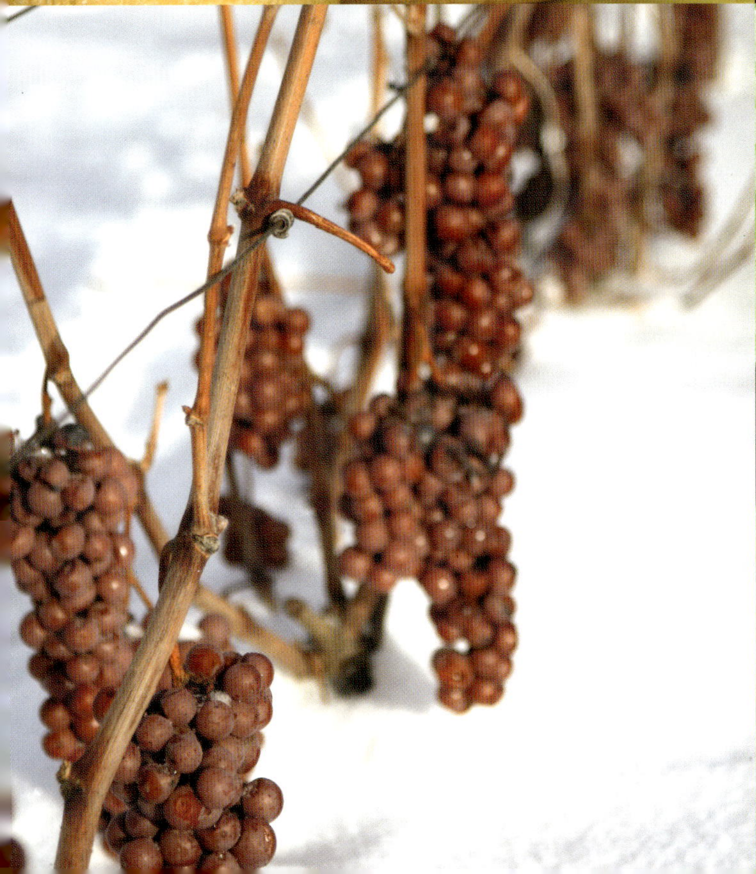
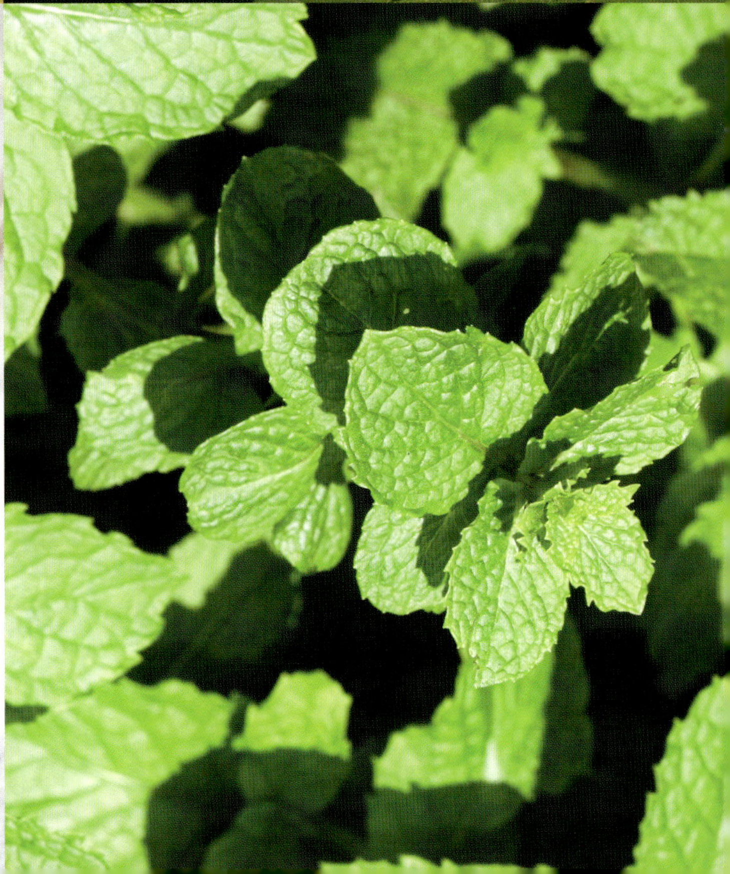

Flavours of a Region *Eastern Townships*

For more regional treats:

LES SUCRERIES DE L'ÉRABLE
16 Rue Principale, Frelighsburg   450-298-5181

LA RUMEUR AFFAMÉE AND LES SUCRERIES DE L'ÉRABLE
3809 Rue Principale, Dunham
15 Rue Principale N., Sutton

LE PETIT DANVILLOIS
12 Rue Du Carmel, Danville   819-839-3636

For more addresses, visit
www.cantonsdelest.com/agrotourisme
produitsdelaferme.com
www.laroutedesvins.ca

Flavours of a Region Eastern Townships

MEGAN SELINE AND STEVEN BEYROUTY
AUBERGE GEORGEVILLE 1889
Georgeville

Megan Seline and Steven Beyrouty bought this quaint, romantic inn in 1996. Built in 1889, the hotel originally opened as summer accommodation for guests traveling by steamboat on Lake Memphremagog, and by stagecoach.

Steven, born in Montreal, has a German mother and an Egyptian father. He remembers his grandmother's cooking—his first inspiration—as well as his mother's. "Like many students, I worked in a restaurant to earn my way through school. I liked cooking enough to make it my trade."

After studying at the Institut de tourisme et d'hôtellerie in Montreal, he worked for a few good establishments in American cities. This gave him a chance to watch good cooks at work and to rediscover the richness of the flavours in Eastern and Asian cuisines.

He settled in the region 15 years ago. He worked at Hovey Manor for four years, and then he and Megan began looking for a house with a history. "Then I heard that the owners of the Georgeville were thinking of retiring.

"At first we had a conventional menu. Then we saw that we had the opportunity to create a more refined cuisine, which needs regional products. I work with several producers who supply deer or cheeses, among other things; I even have a gardener who produces organic vegetables exclusively for us.

"Every year in February, it's a ritual: we meet to go over what has already been on the menu, to discuss new additions, and to determine what we will need for the next summer season."

Steven, who enjoys piloting a small aircraft in his free time, would not change a thing about his life or the path he took to get here. "If I had to do it over again, I would like things to happen the same way. Everything happened at the right time."

See recipes pages 84, 96 and 104

Flavours of a Region *Eastern Townships*

Maryse Carrier and Dominic Tremblay
Café Massawippi
North Hatley

I first met Maryse Carrier and Dominic Tremblay about ten years ago. Although young, they were already exciting chefs, creating dynamic and exotic dishes with style. They were natural cooks, and it seemed that they had already unlocked all the secrets of the kitchen.

Dominic not only makes plans—sometimes rather ambitious ones—he also carries them out. By the age of 23, he was already chef and owner of Café Massawippi, and he has now been there for nearly 10 years. Maryse shares the kitchen tasks with him, balancing out his strengths with her rationality, meticulousness, and skill.

Maryse prefers to focus on preparing and cooking meats; Dominic, for his part, excels in leading gustatory adventures down new and unconventional avenues. He is a good sauce chef, and he sees to it that the food is perfectly cooked. The partners complement each other very well, making it easy for them to run their restaurant and catering business smoothly.

Dominic became captivated with cooking when he was 14 years old, and by the time he was 17 he had decided to seek formal training. The future looked bright, and indeed, it wasn't long before he started reaping the rewards of his new life: while attending Le Triolet school in Sherbrooke and learning the basics of his future trade, he met Maryse. Today they have two beautiful children, Gabrielle and Félix, and a never-ending list of projects.

Dominic first worked in Coaticook, where he was born, and then in Pointe-au-Pic and at La Camarine in Sainte-Anne-de-Beaupré. Maryse grew up in Disraëli in the Chaudière-Appalaches region and has cooked at Auberge Hatley and Laurie-Raphaël restaurant in Quebec City.

Dominic and Maryse have a deep respect for local producers and use only the best products available in the Eastern Townships in their kitchen every day. Their attachment to local products, however, does not prevent them from taking inspiration from other continents to create exotic gourmet experiences.

The young, audacious cuisine at Café Massawippi is a celebration of flavours.

See recipes pages 62, 80 and 102

Flavours of a Region *Eastern Townships*

Stéphane Charpentier
Auberge & Spa West Brome
West Brome

Stéphane Charpentier has been working in the kitchen at the Auberge West Brome since the spring of 2004, and he could not be happier. The size of the business suits him perfectly. Here, he can be a chef "à la française"; that is, he can oversee all aspects of the business, manage personnel, take care of purchasing, and above all, cook every day. In his view, only one in fifty restaurants in Quebec are like that, and most of them are in the regions, away from the cities.

Where does his taste for cooking come from? "I think it is genetic. My paternal grandmother and one of her daughters were wonderful cooks. After high school, I considered going into a career involving water and forestry, working in the woods. But then I had a sudden realization that my calling was to become a chef. Before I came to Quebec, I was lucky to work in a number of two-star restaurants (according to the Michelin Guide) in France."

After arriving here, Stéphane worked at Le Saint-Christophe restaurant in Laval. But he loves the countryside and is very happy here. "I would not go back to France. I like the mentality here; people are calmer, more serene."

Stéphane is originally from Nice and, not surprisingly, he specializes in Provençal cuisine—using local products, of course. "Provençal cuisine has strong tastes and flavours, but I round out the edges a bit to suit the local clientele."

The chef appreciates the contribution of local producers. "I recognize the efforts they have to make to survive. They have to offer the best quality products and outstanding service. Here, there is no problem with supplies since they come to us. They bring mushrooms picked that same morning, wonderful cheeses, and their good humour. I talk to them every week, and it ends up feeling very much like a family."

See recipes pages 50, 88 and 106

Patricia Provencher and Hans Christiner
Auberge du Joli Vent
Lac Brome

Hans Christiner explains it simply: "Love brought me to Quebec!" Born in Lucerne, Switzerland, he met Patricia when they both lived in Australia. "She is from the Eastern Townships, and she convinced me to come back with her to see the beautiful Quebec winters."

Patricia Provencher, an endocrinologist, was doing post-doctoral work in Australia. Through friends—all of them foodies—she met Hans, who was working at the Swiss Club in Melbourne.

They came to Quebec in 1994, and Patricia taught at the faculty of medicine of Sherbrooke University. At the time, they both dreamed about moving closer to nature, to an inn in the country. In 2000, their brilliant idea became a reality when they purchased a beautiful 19th century inn and took over the business.

Today, Patricia manages the inn while Hans expresses his creativity in the kitchen. He has been influenced by his travels to Australia, Saudi Arabia, and New Zealand, and his cuisine, while not exclusively Swiss, is solid and uses only local products.

L'Auberge du Joli Vent is also a family business. "For the moment, our sons Timothé and Félix appreciate good food as consumers, not artisans! But they can already make great fried eggs!"

Here, the excellent regional cheeses are always available. "Cheese makers come to sell them to us and we are proud to let our customers discover them."

Far away from the hubbub of the kitchen, the beautiful colours in the chef's garden and the flowers further on whisper invitations to take a stroll and soak in the beauty of the surroundings.

See recipes pages 72, 82 and 110

Flavours of a Region *Eastern Townships*

François Dubois
Le Bocage
Compton

Just outside Compton, on Moe's River Road, you will find François Dubois welcoming guests to his beautiful Victorian house, originally built in 1825. Spend a little time there, and you will see that the garden, the house as a whole, and the dining room are places where time seems to stand still.

François purchased Le Bocage in 1997, and decided to keep it up as an inn. Renovations were not even necessary, since the bedrooms, kitchen, and everything else were in impeccable condition.

François had been working in the restaurant business for a long time, although he had more experience in service than in the kitchen. He had been developing his cooking talents as a hobby for some time, however, and decided to dive in headfirst by purchasing the inn and putting himself to work.

Some may feel that Le Bocage is in the middle of nowhere. Quite the contrary, however, as the location gives François access to a large number of producers in Compton and the area. And just as he takes great pleasure in cooking with local products, so do local producers enjoy collaborating with the chef.

"Local products are a distinguishing characteristic of the region. Look at the diversity! Compton has more than apples, pears, and berries, it also has cheeses, butter, cream…. These are real, authentic products."

There is no need to keep a huge garden, since there is an abundance of excellent vegetables grown in the region. Nevertheless, François likes to grow his own herbs and edible flowers.

He prefers to offer dishes that people tend not to prepare at home, adding an exotic touch to his menus to please the food lovers. As he says, "My cuisine is all about pleasure. Pleasure in conception, in preparation, in serving, and of course, in tasting." In the intimate environment of Le Bocage, François serves meals he prepares lovingly for his guests and does everything he can to make them as comfortable as possible.

See recipes pages 54, 90 and 100

ALAIN LABRIE
GROUPE GERMAIN

Alain Labrie studied in the Gaspésie region at Fort-Prével, a school associated with a hotel where the students were encouraged to put their techniques into practice as soon as possible. He has worked in Saguenay, in the Baie des Chaleurs region, and in Montreal.

In 1989, he joined the Auberge Hatley team. It took him only six months to climb to the position of chef de cuisine. He then became the executive chef, a position he held along with food and beverage manager until 2006, when the inn was destroyed by fire.

Alain has always loved quality products. "Take aromatic herbs: Micheline, the gardener, would tell me about her latest discoveries, and we would create dishes with what was growing in the garden. We worked like that for 15 years.

"When the first local products became available, our experiments were not always successful and the quality was sometimes uneven. Still, we had a duty to use them and make them known, and our restaurant was a good place to do this. We would experiment and have a dialogue going with the producers, and this helped them improve their products. I have always respected them; they work as much as I do. We have to collaborate intelligently, and I am here to do that. I've worked hard too, and I've learned. I had never seen foie gras before I had to cook one at the Auberge."

Alain worked with young gardeners from Lennoxville. He did not buy the vegetables because they were organic, he bought them because they were perfect. "The same thing applies to Ferme de Cerf de Highwater or Lapins de Stanstead."

Although the Auberge Hatley has disappeared, Alain is still cooking. He takes part in public events and teaches his employees. "They are people who work for me, but above all with me. We all have something to learn from each other."

See recipes pages 70 and 78

Flavours of a Region *Eastern Townships*

Roland Ménard
Hovey Manor
North Hatley

At 14, Roland Ménard got a job at a family-type restaurant in Magog. One year later, he was cooking. "I was immediately captivated. The owner was afraid to lose his clientele, so he forbade his staff from telling anyone that a 'kid' was cooking. I worked there for nine years. I think it's in my blood."

His second job at the Hovey Manor is his "home", where he spends 12 hours every day. "In the 27 years I've worked here, I've had so many opportunities to develop my own tastes and to translate them into my cooking. I'm self-taught, and I'm very comfortable with combining ingredients. Even today, I start a new recipe by writing it down, and then I test it. I don't make too many mistakes.

"I read of course, and I write, but nature is my main source of inspiration. I like to touch, to see vegetables grow in the garden, to smell a tomato on the vine. Then I take a piece of paper and…."

Roland takes the time to visit local producers on a regular basis, and he brings his team with him. It is important to see how an organic farm operates on a day-to-day basis. "The dialogue encourages us to exceed our own limits, both at the farm and in the kitchen. There is no such thing as a miracle. We can't create delicious dishes if the local producers don't support us. We promote the best products not for the way they look but for the way they taste."

Roland waited patiently for changes in the supply network. In his case, he began working with local producers and has been doing so for about twenty years now. Some have been his suppliers since the beginning.

Roland's talent has always impressed, and he has several awards to prove it. He is a chef happy in his work, so immersed that he does not see the time go by. And when he gets an idea, he simply takes a piece of paper, writes it down, and voilà! A new recipe is born!

See recipes pages 52, 60 and 108

JACQUES POULIN
CHÂTEAU BROMONT
Bromont

Jacques Poulin is a man whose deep roots in the Eastern Townships are rivalled only by his love of the area. In his opinion, this region has the best local products in all of Quebec. Of course, he has been to see how things are done elsewhere, but he has found nothing to equal the enthusiasm of the producers here, especially over the last five years. "It is phenomenal to see how refined products are multiplying as fast as the quality improves."

Jacques has spent most of his career in a few good establishments in the Eastern Townships, except when he worked at the Ritz Carlton in Montreal and in the kitchen at Rideau Hall in Ottawa.

He is now executive chef at Château Bromont, a challenging and exciting position. In this restaurant, the menu reflects the philosophy behind the cuisine.

This chef appreciates what he calls "comfort food." "For me, it's simple cuisine, but not commonplace. It means perfectly cooked food, united with harmonious aromas and flavours. A good meal is like a rest, which we all need to take once in a while. I enjoy looking at a dish for a few moments before I begin to savour the food. I don't like plates that are overloaded, but I do like colours that accentuate the flavours."

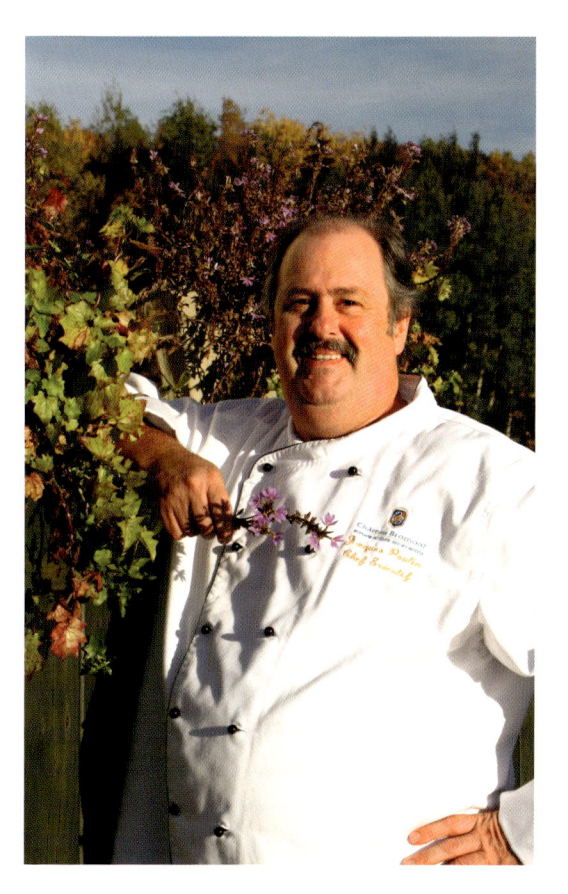

Jacques enjoys talking to artisan producers, to whom a professional chef's knowledge can be useful. In order to sell their products to the consumers, they often have to suggest cooking methods, not always an easy task when their products are bison, deer, or duck, for instance. "We can also work with less popular cuts, such as braised jowls, shanks for osso bucco, or braised cross-rib in duck fat.

"In these types of exchanges, we all come out winners."

See recipes pages 68 and 92

Flavours of a Region *Eastern Townships*

Martine and Patrick Satre
Le temps des cerises Restaurant
Danville

Martine is from Belgium, Patrick is from France, and they met in Switzerland. In 1980, intrigued by the possibilities they saw opening up in Quebec, they moved here. Patrick worked in hotel management for a major hotel chain in Montreal.

In the late 1980s, they left the city behind to settle in Danville, where they purchased the Saint Andrew church and converted it into a restaurant. With four years of study in restaurant techniques in Namur and hotel management in Lausanne, Switzerland, and after teaching cooking to children and giving courses at Lasalle College in Montreal, Martine had begun to think seriously about cooking for her own clients.

"At the time, all we needed were a few good dishes and the clients were happy. Although our project was hard work at the beginning, local suppliers were always good allies and we grew gradually. The cuisine evolved with our clientele."

Today, Patrick is responsible for serving the customers and for wine and cheese supplies. He also oversees the management of the restaurant. Martine cooks and sees to décor and promotion.

"I enjoy cooking with local products. The quality is excellent and sometimes certain products are exclusive. I buy about 50 naturally raised lambs from Ferme Manasan. They are the right weight, they have an excellent yield, and the quality is beyond reproach. The pickers come to me with fiddleheads and mushrooms. Other artisans sell us their berries, cheese, and flour. We can go a long way with the producers!"

For Martine, logistics is the first step towards inspiration. In the tiny kitchen, she performs small miracles. We are in a church, after all.

On the lower floor, there is a beautiful and much larger kitchen that is used for workshops and to make chutney from cranberries and yellow beets, as well as the other delicious preserves that are sold on the premises.

See recipes pages 64, 66 and 76

Flavours of a Region Eastern Townships

James Stearns
Auberge Les Victorines du Lac
Lac-Mégantic

At Christmastime, the young James Stearns used to visit his grandmother, a cordon bleu cook, to help bake and decorate shortbread cookies. "That is when my love for cooking began. I have travelled extensively, I own several cookbooks, and I have worked in a kitchen all my life."

Born in Lac-Mégantic, James left to travel the world at the age of 17. He worked in Jasper, in Montreal, and even in Australia. In Miami, where he worked with Simon Bernard at L'Alouette, he developed a taste for refined cuisine. He trained with Charles Barrier at Le Nègre in Tours, France, and has also worked with James McGuire at Passe-Partout in Montreal. He was also in Ontario at Langdon Hall, a member of the prestigious *Relais et Châteaux*.

The chef learned his trade in some of the planet's best kitchens. Although his ambitions were lofty, he has attained them thanks to his travelling and reading and, most important, his devotion to his work.

He returned to Lac-Mégantic in 2000, and declares, "My travels are over! Except for vacations." Now married with two children, it is safe to say that he has settled down for good in the land of his forefathers. James loves fishing and hunting, and has everything he could wish for in this beautiful environment.

James feels that he has a duty to encourage the artisan producers of the Lac-Mégantic region. He recognizes their talent and perseverance and proudly includes their names on the menu. "There may not be as many local producers here as in other regions, but that also has its good side. It lets us build a closer relationship with them. We literally get the cream of the crop."

James has shown that it is possible to create outstanding cuisine made entirely from products from the Lac-Mégantic region.

See recipes pages 56, 86 and 98

SANCTUAIRE St.ANTOINE

Flavours of a Region *Eastern Townships*

Recipes

Flavours of a Region *Eastern Townships*

Soups

CREAM OF SQUASH AND BRISE DU VIGNERON FROM FROMAGERIE DES CANTONS
Stéphane Charpentier, *Auberge West Brome*

YELLOW TOMATO GAZPACHO FROM SANDERS FARM
Roland Ménard, *Hovey Manor*

POTAGE EN DUO BEET FROM VALLONS MARAÎCHERS AND APPLE FROM VERGER LE GROS PIERRE
François Dubois, *Le Bocage*

VELOUTÉ OF ASPARAGUS
James Stearns, *Auberge Les Victorines du Lac*

The Eastern Townships is an exceptional wine region, unrivalled in all of Quebec. In celebration of this fact, each recipe is accompanied by a suggestion for wine or cider to complement the regional products.

Note: The soup-wine symbiosis is an extremely delicate one. Suggestions are nevertheless included to tempt the more adventurous gastronomes.

Philippe Lapeyrie, sommelier

49

Flavours of a Region *Eastern Townships*

CREAM OF SQUASH AND BRISE DU VIGNERON
FROM FROMAGERIE DES CANTONS

Peel squash, remove seeds, and dice coarsely.

In a saucepan, melt butter over medium heat and add leek and onion. Add a pinch of salt, pepper, and sugar. Cover and steam for a few minutes.

Add squash and moisten with stock. Bring to a boil. Add rice, then cover and simmer for approximately 35 minutes.

Purée in a blender, then strain through a chinois. Add cream and season.

Lightly toast slices of bread in the oven. Remove, add a piece of cheese on top, drizzle with olive oil, and return to a very hot oven for a few seconds.

Serves 4

1	1.8 kg (4 lb) butternut squash	
1	large leek, white portion, finely chopped	
1	large onion, finely chopped	
45 mL	butter	3 tablespoons
1.25 L	poultry broth	5 cups
60 mL	rice	1/4 cup
185 mL	35% cream	3/4 cup
	salt, pepper, sugar	
4	slices of baguette bread	
150 g	Brise du Vigneron cheese	5 1/2 ounces
2.5 mL	extra virgin olive oil	1/2 teaspoon

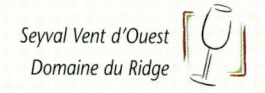

Seyval Vent d'Ouest
Domaine du Ridge

See Fromagerie des Cantons page 27

Flavours of a Region *Eastern Townships*

Flavours of a Region *Eastern Townships*

YELLOW TOMATO GAZPACHO
FROM SANDERS FARM

Flavours of a Region *Eastern Townships*

In a bowl, mix garlic, oil, vinegar, and salt. Add tomatoes and refrigerate for 24 hours.

Add remaining ingredients. Purée in a blender, then strain through a chinois. Season and refrigerate.

In a skillet, melt butter over medium heat and add herbs. Raise heat and sauté cubes of bread until golden.

Serve cold.

Serves 4

500 g	yellow tomatoes, seeded	1 pound 2 ounces
1	clove garlic, finely chopped	
7.5 mL	olive oil	1/2 tablespoon
20 mL	white wine vinegar	4 teaspoons
2.5 mL	coarse salt	1/2 teaspoon
500 mL	water	2 cups
1/4	fennel bulb	
1/4	Spanish onion, finely chopped	
1/4	English cucumber, peeled and diced	
1/2	yellow pepper, seeded and diced	
2.5 mL	Worcestershire sauce	1/2 teaspoon
2 drops	Tabasco	

Herb croutons

125 mL	white bread, crusts removed and cubed	1/2 cup
45 mL	butter	3 tablespoons
2.5 mL	dry herbs	1/2 teaspoon

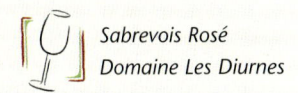

Sabrevois Rosé
Domaine Les Diurnes

See Ferme Sanders page 123

53

Flavours of a Region *Eastern Townships*

POTAGE EN DUO
BEET FROM VALLONS MARAÎCHERS
AND APPLE FROM VERGER LE GROS PIERRE

Serves 4

Cream of beet

6	medium size beets, coarsely diced	
15 mL	olive oil	1 tablespoon
1	onion, diced	
1	clove garlic, finely chopped	
15 mL	red wine vinegar	1 tablespoon
1 L	poultry broth	4 cups
	salt and pepper	

Pour olive oil into a saucepan and sweat onion and garlic. Season. Add beets and cook for 1 minute. Deglaze with vinegar. Moisten with broth. Simmer for 45 minutes or until beets are tender. Purée in a blender, then strain through a chinois. Reserve.

Cream of apples

4	large Cortland apples, peeled and cut in wedges	
	lemon juice	
1	onion, diced	
1	clove garlic, finely chopped	
15 mL	olive oil	1 tablespoon
1	potato, diced	
1 L	poultry broth	4 cups
60 mL	35% cream	1/4 cup
	salt and pepper	

Drizzle lemon juice over the apple wedges. Reserve.

Pour olive oil into a saucepan and sweat onion and garlic. Season. Add apples and potato and moisten with broth. Simmer for 25 minutes. Purée in a blender, then strain through a chinois. Reheat and add cream.

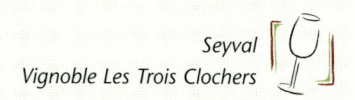

Seyval
Vignoble Les Trois Clochers

See Vallons Maraîchers page 125
See Verger Le Gros Pierre page 125

Flavours of a Region *Eastern Townships*

VELOUTÉ OF ASPARAGUS

Serves 6

900 g	fresh asparagus	2 pounds
1	white Spanish onion, finely chopped	
15 mL	butter	1 tablespoon
75 mL	flour	5 tablespoons
1 L	poultry broth	4 cups
200 mL	35% cream	3/4 cup
	salt and pepper	

Cut asparagus into pieces, keeping a few spears for garnish.

Melt butter in a saucepan and sauté onion. Add asparagus and sweat. Singe with flour and moisten with broth. Simmer for approximately 40 minutes.

Purée in a blender, then strain through a chinois. Reheat and add cream. Season.

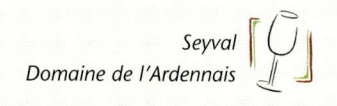

Seyval
Domaine de l'Ardennais

Flavours of a Region *Eastern Townships*

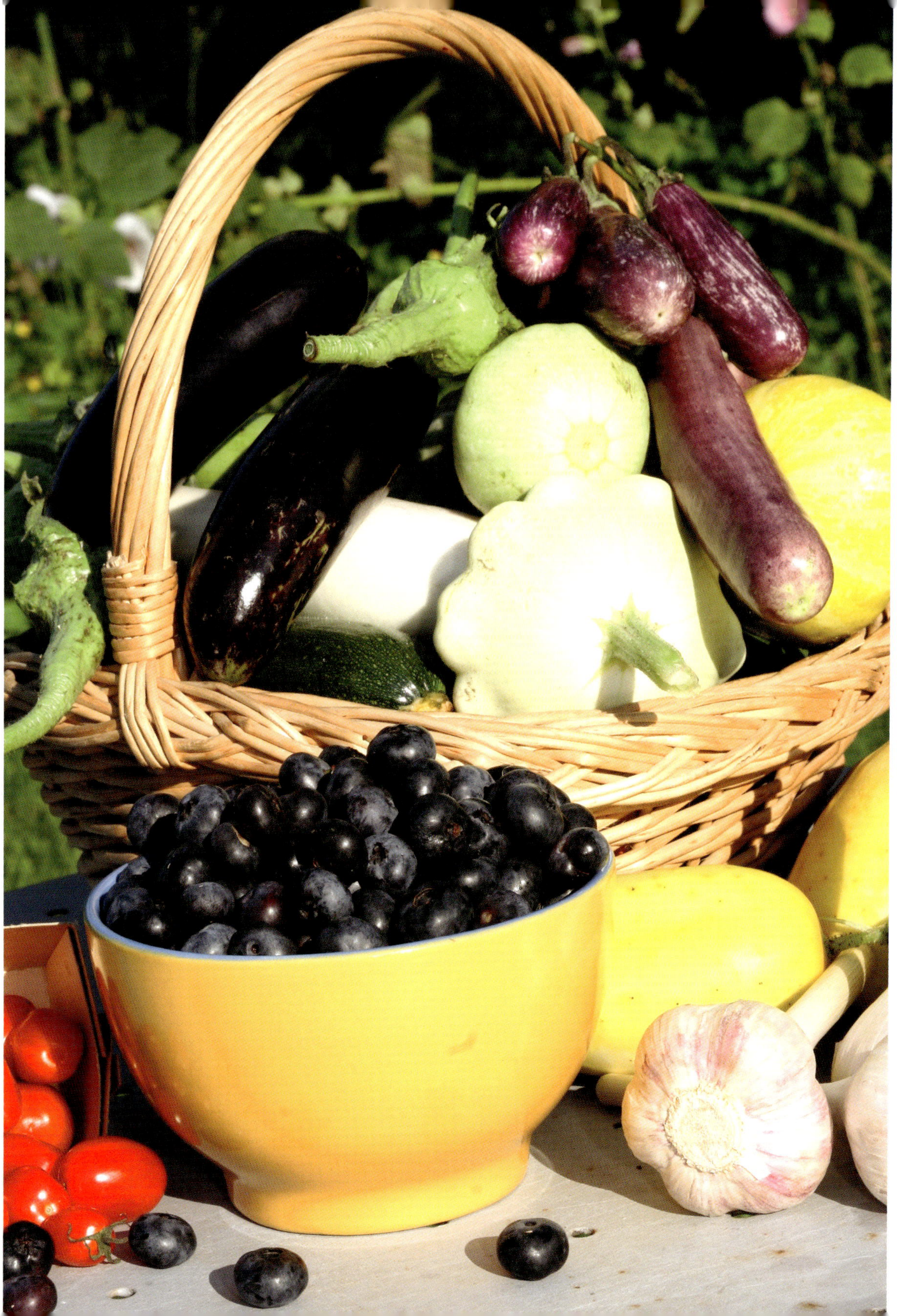

Appetizers

BRAISED PORK JOWLS AGNOLOTTI WITH MOÛT DE P.O.M.
BOUDIN NOIR À LA NORMANDE
Roland Ménard – *Hovey Manor*

CAPRICE DES CANTONS FROM FROMAGERIE LA GERMAINE
LAVENDER FROM BLEU LAVANDE AND HONEY FONDANT
Dominic Tremblay – *Café Massawippi*

FIDDLEHEAD FLAN FROM PRODUITS INDIGÈNES
GOAT CHEESE TUILE
Martine Satre – *Le temps des cerises*

DUCK PASTILLA FROM BONTÉS DIVINES
CRANBERRY CHUTNEY
Martine Satre – *Le temps des cerises*

POACHED PEAR, DUCK FOIE GRAS FROM BONTÉS DIVINES
LAKE BROME DUCK LIVERS AND ARCHER FROM CEP D'ARGENT
Jacques Poulain – *Château Bromont*

PRESSÉ OF RABBIT FROM LAPINS DE STANSTEAD
AND DUCK FOIE GRAS FROM DUCS DE MONTRICHARD
Alain Labrie – *Groupe Germain*

SWISS CHARD SPÄTZLI AND
TOMME DES JOYEUX FROMAGERS GRATIN
FROM CHÈVRERIE FRUIT D'UNE PASSION
Hans Christiner – *Auberge du Joli Vent*

Flavours of a Region *Eastern Townships*

BRAISED PORK JOWLS AGNOLOTTI WITH MOÛT DE P.O.M.
BOUDIN NOIR À LA NORMANDE

12 agnolotti

2	500 g (1 lb 2 oz) pork jowls	
1/2	Spanish onion, finely diced	
1/2	carrot, finely diced	
1	stalk celery, finely diced	
1/2	clove garlic, minced	
1	sprig of thyme	
1/2	bay leaf	
1	cinnamon stick	
185 mL	Moût de P.O.M.	3/4 cup
500 mL	brown stock	4 cups
310 mL	poultry broth	1 1/4 cup
30 mL	butter	2 tablespoons
	salt and pepper	

Boudin

200 g	boudin noir (black pudding)	7 ounces
1	apple, cut in wedges	
30 mL	butter	2 tablespoons

In a small ovenproof casserole, melt butter, sear pork jowls on all sides. Add onions, carrots, celery, and herbs. Deglaze with Moût de pomme, then cook in a preheated oven at 180°C (350°F) for approximately 4 hours.

Remove meat from bones, dice finely, and reserve. Strain cooking juices through a chinois. Cool until fat congeals. Skim and discard fat.

Pour liquid into a saucepan, then add meat and stock. Reduce cooking juices until almost dry. Season.

With fresh pasta dough, make agnolotti. Cut 8 x 6 cm (3 1/8 x 2 1/4 in) rectangles and place a small amount of braised meat in the centre. Seal. Poach agnolotti in poultry broth.

Cut boudin and sauté in butter. Brown apple wedges and place on top of boudin. Serve with poultry broth.

Vidal
Vignoble La Mission

See Moûts de P.O.M. page 125

Flavours of a Region *Eastern Townships*

Flavours of a Region *Eastern Townships*

CAPRICE DES CANTONS FROM FROMAGERIE LA GERMAINE
LAVANDER FROM BLEU LAVANDE AND HONEY FONDANT

Flavours of a Region *Eastern Townships*

In a non-stick skillet, heat sugar until golden. Combine fruits (apple, pear, and plum). Simmer for approximately 3 minutes, then pour in the tea syrup and cool in the refrigerator.

Pour honey and lavender into a microwave safe bowl. Heat for a few moments until the lavender releases its full flavour.

Pour water into a saucepan. Add sugar and tea leaves, and heat to a simmer. Strain through a chinois and refrigerate.

Cut cheese into 4 equal parts and put into ramekins. Drizzle with lavender honey and warm in a preheated 180°C (350°F) oven for 2 or 3 minutes.

Serves 4

250 g	Caprices des Cantons cheese	9 ounces
1	apple, thinly sliced	
1	pear, thinly sliced	
1	plum, thinly sliced	
30 mL	sugar	2 tablespoons
60 mL	liquid honey	1/4 cup
15 mL	lavender	1 tablespoon

Tea syrup

125 mL	water	1/2 cup
60 mL	sugar	1/4 cup
60 mL	green tea leaves	1/4 cup

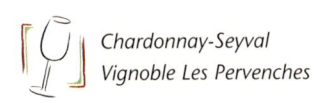

Chardonnay-Seyval
Vignoble Les Pervenches

See Fromagerie La Germaine page 123
See Bleu Lavande page 28

Flavours of a Region *Eastern Townships*

FIDDLEHEAD FLAN FROM PRODUITS INDIGÈNES
GOAT CHEESE TUILE

Flavours of a Region *Eastern Townships*

In a saucepan, combine milk, cream, onion, garlic, salt, and pepper. Add fiddleheads. Bring to a boil. Purée in a blender. Reserve.

Using a fork, beat eggs and egg yolks. Blend into the mixture.

Pour equal portions into ramekins. Place ramekins in a dripping-pan half-filled with water. Cook in a preheated 180°C (350°F) oven. Serve warm.

Line a cookie sheet with non-stick paper. Shape cheese into 8 cm (3 1/8 in) diameter circles, leaving a 1.5 cm (5/8 in) space between each to allow for spreading. Bake tuiles in a preheated 190°C (375°F) oven for approximately 10 minutes.

Serves 8

300 g	fiddleheads	10 1/2 ounces
150 mL	milk	5/8 cup
150 mL	35% cream	5/8 cup
1/2	onion, finely chopped	
1	clove garlic, finely chopped	
3	eggs	
2	egg yolks	
	salt and pepper	

Tuile

160 g	grated goat cheddar cheese	5 3/4 ounces

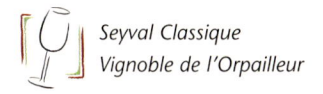

Seyval Classique
Vignoble de l'Orpailleur

See Produits Indigènes page 125

DUCK PASTILLA FROM BONTÉS DIVINES
CRANBERRY CHUTNEY

Serves 6

500 g	duck confit	1 pound 2 ounces
100 g	almond powder	3 1/2 ounces
5 mL	cinnamon	1 teaspoon
100 mL	poultry broth	3/8 cup
3 sheets	phyllo pastry	
45 mL	melted butter	3 tablespoons
	icing sugar	

Chutney

500 g	fresh cranberries	1 pound 2 ounces
1/2	onion, finely chopped	
150 mL	vinegar	5/8 cup
100 mL	brown sugar	3/8 cup
1	bay leaf	
1.25 mL	ground cinnamon	1/4 teaspoon
1.25 mL	ground ginger	1/4 teaspoon
1.25 mL	grated nutmeg	1/4 teaspoon
	salt and pepper	

Break up duck confit. Mix in almond powder and cinnamon. Moisten the mixture with poultry broth.

Cut sheets of phyllo pastry into four parts. With a pastry brush, brush sheets of phyllo with melted butter. Stack crosswise. Spread equal portions of duck meat in the centre of each pastilla. Seal phyllo pastry, shaping it into a cylinder. Bake in a preheated 190°C (375°F) oven for approximately 20 minutes. To garnish, dust each pastilla with cinnamon and icing sugar.

Mix all the ingredients in a saucepan and bring to a boil. Simmer for approximately 20 minutes. Reserve.

Haute Combe
Domaine des Côtes d'Ardoise

See Bontés Divines page 21

Flavours of a Region *Eastern Townships*

POACHED PEAR, DUCK FOIE GRAS FROM BONTÉS DIVINES
LAKE BROME DUCK LIVERS AND ARCHER FROM CEP D'ARGENT

Serves 4

Pears

4	pears, peeled	
80 mL	linden tea	1/3 cup
2 L	boiling water	8 cups

Foie gras and livers

120 g	duck livers	4 ounces
90 g	lobe of duck foie gras	3 ounces
200 mL	flour with salt, pepper, and mustard powder	3/4 cup
45 mL	duck fat	3 tablespoons
160 mL	Archer wine	2/3 cup
4	slices of whole wheat baguette bread, toasted	

In a saucepan, steep linden tea in boiling water for 20 minutes. Poach pears in linden tea for 20 minutes. Remove pears and cool in the refrigerator for approximately 5 minutes.

Cut pears in half and remove cores. Reserve.

Trim and dredge duck livers in flour.

In a skillet, melt duck fat and sauté livers. Reserve.

Finely mince livers and foie gras. Mix well while moistening with Archer wine.

Make 4 patties and sear them in the skillet until slightly brown. Place a patty on each slice of bread.

Place bread and patty on the base of the pear and cover with the top half.

Bring Archer wine to a boil and thicken with a small amount of cornstarch if necessary.

Vendange tardive, Sélection Camille
Vignoble de la Bauge

See Bontés Divines page 21
See Canards du Lac Brome page 28
See Vignoble Le Cep d'Argent page 125

Flavours of a Region *Eastern Townships*

PRESSÉ OF RABBIT FROM LAPINS DE STANSTEAD AND DUCK FOIE GRAS FROM DUCS DE MONTRICHARD

Serves 6

400 g	lobe of duck foie gras	14 ounces
350 g	rabbit confit	12 ounces
30 mL	cognac	2 tablespoons
60 mL	ice cider	1/4 cup
10 mL	fresh parsley, chopped	2 teaspoons
10 mL	fresh chives, chopped	2 teaspoons
5 mL	fresh tarragon, chopped	1 teaspoon
10 mL	shallots, minced	2 teaspoons
5 mL	sherry vinegar	1 teaspoon
45 mL	duck fat	3 tablespoons
45 mL	duck stock, reduced	3 tablespoons
	salt, Tabasco and Worcestershire sauce	

Trim lobe of foie gras and macerate in cognac and ice cider. Place in a small dripping pan and cook in a preheated 140 °C (275 °F) oven for approximately 18 minutes. Cool and pat dry.

Mix rabbit confit with herbs, shallots, vinegar, duck fat, and stock. Season.

Alternate layers of foie gras and rabbit in a terrine mould. Cool in the refrigerator for 12 hours.

Riesling
Domaine des Côtes d'Ardoise

See Lapins de Stanstead page 123
See Ducs de Montrichard page 123

Flavours of a Region *Eastern Townships*

SWISS CHARD SPÄTZLI AND TOMME DES JOYEUX FROMAGERS GRATIN FROM CHÈVRERIE FRUIT D'UNE PASSION

Combine all ingredients in a bowl, except for the Swiss chard. Knead the dough until smooth. Let stand for 30 minutes. Add the Swiss chard and beat vigorously.

In a pot, bring a large amount of salted water to a boil. Reduce heat. Press the dough vigorously through a spätzli sieve over the saucepan. Simmer the spätzli until they float to the surface. Remove with a skimmer and cool quickly under cold running water.

Melt butter in a skillet and sauté the chanterelles. Add the spätzli and warm thoroughly. Season. Pour into a gratin dish and sprinkle cheese evenly on top. Brown in a preheated 195°C (380°F) oven.

Serves 4

Spätzli

200 g	blanched Swiss chard leaves, minced	7 ounces
500 mL	flour	2 cups
2	eggs	
15 mL	milk	1 tablespoon
15 mL	semolina	1 tablespoon
	salt	

Gratin

320 g	fresh chanterelles, cleaned	10 3/4 ounces
120 g	goat cheese, diced	4 ounces
15 mL	butter	1 tablespoon
	salt and pepper	

Seyval La Taste
Vignoble Les Blancs Côteaux

See Chèvrerie Fruit d'une Passion page 24

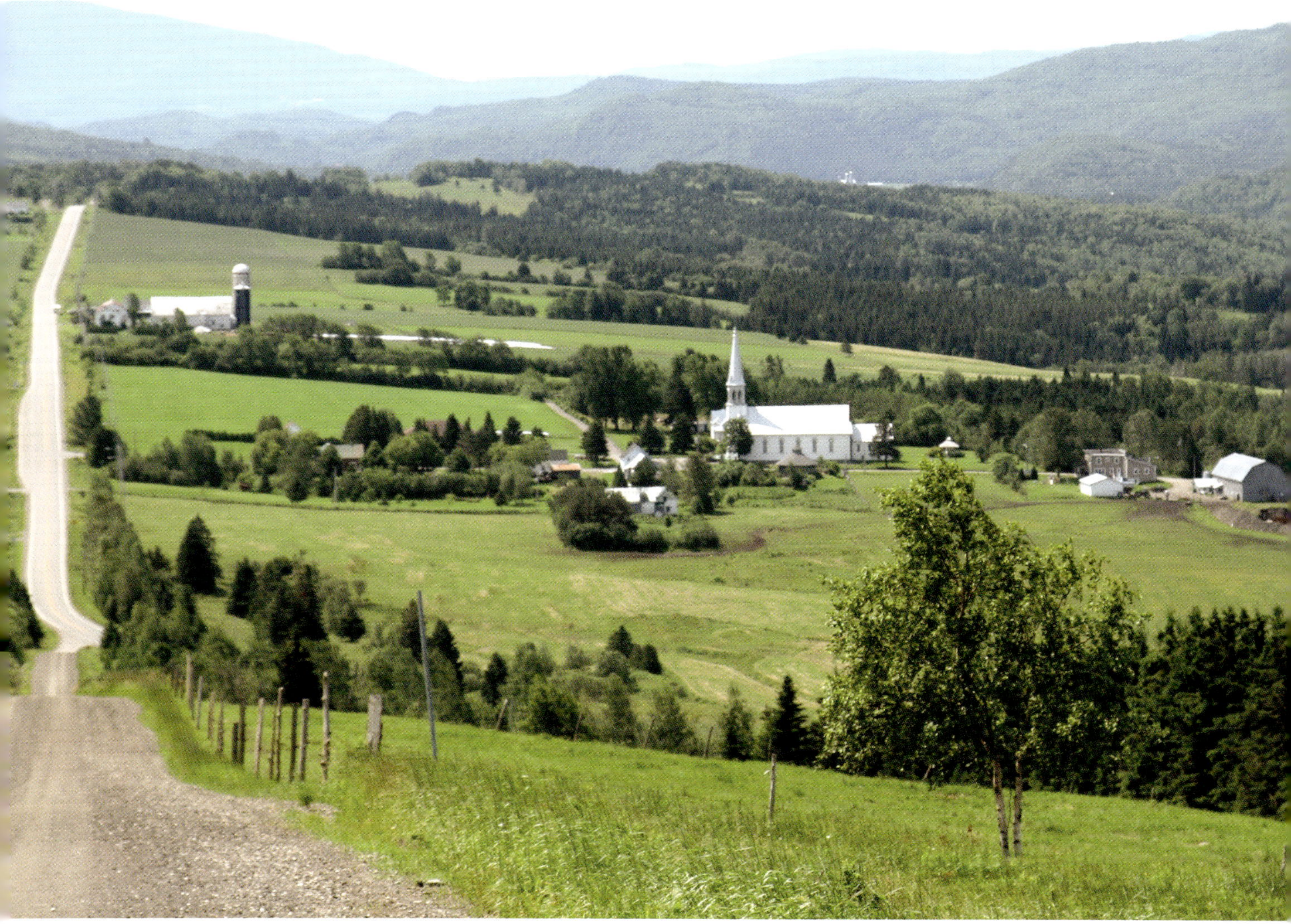

Main Dishes

BRAISED LAMB FROM FERME MANASAN
Martine Satre – *Le temps des cerises*

RIB OF CERF DE HIGHWATER AND SHANK CONFIT
EGGPLANT AND ALFRED LE FERMIER GRATIN
FROM FROMAGERIE LA STATION
Alain Labrie – *Groupe Germain*

DUCK FOIE GRAS FROM BONTÉS DIVINES
APPLES FROM VERGER LE GROS PIERRE
Dominic Tremblay – *Café Massawippi*

LEG OF GOAT FROM CHÈVRERIE FRUIT D'UNE PASSION
POLENTA AND ROASTED RED PEPPERS
Hans Christiner – *Auberge du Joli Vent*

LOIN OF CERF DE HIGHWATER
CRANBERRY CHUTNEY
Steven Beyrouty – *Auberge Georgeville 1889*

BISON EN PORTEFEUILLE FROM DOMAINE DU BISON
VEGETABLES AND TOMME DES JOYEUX FROMAGERS
FROM CHÈVRERIE FRUIT D'UNE PASSION
James Stearns – *Auberge Les Victorines du Lac*

ROCK CORNISH HEN WITH
RED PEPPER JELLY IN COARSE SALT CRUST
Stéphane Charpentier – *Auberge West Brome*

ROULÉ OF LAPIN DE STANSTEAD
AND APPLES FROM VERGER LE GROS PIERRE
François Dubois – *Le Bocage*

BOBINES TROUT WITH PART DES ANGES FROM L'ORPAILLEUR
ABBAYE DE SAINT-BENOÎT GRUYÈRE PILLOW
Jacques Poulain – *Château Bromont*

Flavours of a Region *Eastern Townships*

BRAISED LAMB FROM FERME MANASAN

Heat olive oil in a large, heavy-bottomed skillet. Sear cubes of lamb on one side without turning. Dredge with flour and turn immediately. Colour the meat (do not cook) and remove. Deglaze with a small amount of red wine and pour the liquid over the meat.

Add garlic and cardamom seeds. Return meat to skillet and cover with remaining wine. Simmer for approximately 1 hour and 15 minutes. Meat should be tender but not separate. Season.

Serves 4

800 g	lamb shoulder or neck, cubed	1 pound 12 ounces
30 mL	olive oil	2 tablespoons
60 mL	flour	1/4 cup
310 mL	red wine	1 1/4 cup
4	cloves garlic, finely chopped	
3 pods	cardamom	
	salt and pepper	

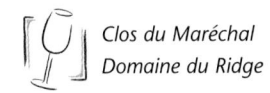

Clos du Maréchal
Domaine du Ridge

See Ferme Manasan page 123

RIB OF CERF DE HIGHWATER AND SHANK CONFIT EGGPLANT AND ALFRED LE FERMIER GRATIN
FROM FROMAGERIE LA STATION

Serves 6

1	1.2 kg (2 lb 9 oz) rack of deer ribs	
30 mL	olive oil	2 tablespoons
15 mL	butter	1 tablespoon

Shank confit

200 g	shank confit	7 ounces
30 mL	shallot, minced	2 tablespoons
60 mL	wild mushrooms, finely chopped	1/4 cup
45 mL	red wine	3 tablespoons
80 mL	juniper sauce	1/3 cup
15 mL	fresh oregano, chopped	1 tablespoon
15 mL	butter	1 tablespoon

Sauce

30 mL	shallot, minced	2 tablespoons
60 mL	white mushrooms, finely chopped	1/4 cup
15 mL	butter	1 tablespoon
50 mL	gin	3 tablespoons + 1 teaspoon
100 mL	red wine	3/8 cup
1 L	game stock	4 cups
1 L	duck stock	4 cups
15 mL	crushed juniper berries	1 tablespoon

Eggplant gratin

6	Italian eggplants	
200 mL	extra virgin oil	3/4 cup
125 g	Alfred le fermier cheese, grated	4 1/2 ounces
250 mL	crushed tomatoes	1 cup
	salt and pepper	

Heat butter and oil in an ovenproof skillet and sear deer ribs on all sides. Cook in a preheated 220°C (425°F) oven for 10 to 15 minutes. Remove from oven and reserve a few minutes. Slice off one rib per person.

In a skillet, melt butter and sweat shallots and mushrooms. Add meat and heat. Deglaze with red wine and thicken with a small amount of sauce. Add oregano.

In a skillet, melt butter and sauté shallots, mushrooms, and two-thirds of the juniper berries. Deglaze with gin and red wine. Moisten with game and duck stock. Reduce to one quarter. Strain through a chinois. Add the remaining juniper berries. Reserve.

Slice eggplants. In a frying pan, sauté in olive oil. Reserve.

Flavours of a Region *Eastern Townships*

Crush tomatoes. In a saucepan, sweat onion and garlic in olive oil. Add tomatoes. Reduce until almost dry. Season and add herbs.

Place slices of eggplant and concassé in alternating layers. Garnish with cheese and bake in a preheated 180°C (350°F) oven for approximately 20 minutes.

Tomato concassé

8	tomatoes blanched, peeled, and seeded	
1	onion, minced	
2	cloves garlic, finely chopped	
30 mL	extra virgin oil	2 tablespoons
1	pinch of sugar	
	salt and pepper	
15 mL	fresh thyme, chopped	1 tablespoon
15 mL	fresh basil, chopped	1 tablespoon

L'Orpailleur Rouge
Vignoble de l'Orpailleur

See Ferme de Cerfs Highwater page 123

See Fromagerie La Station page 30

79

DUCK FOIE GRAS FROM BONTÉS DIVINES
APPLES FROM VERGER LE GROS PIERRE

Serves 4

4	100 g (3 1/2 oz) escalopes of duck foie gras	
2	large Cortland apples	
30 mL	parsley, chopped	2 tablespoons
	fleur de sel	

Maple and balsamic vinaigrette

2	shallots, chopped	
2	cloves garlic, minced	
80 mL	dark maple syrup	1/3 cup
30 mL	balsamic vinegar	2 tablespoons
30 mL	tamari sauce	2 tablespoons
125 mL	olive oil	1/2 cup
	salt and pepper	

With a sharp knife, trace a criss-cross pattern on the escalopes. Place escalopes in a very hot skillet, pattern side down. Sear for approximately 3 minutes on both sides. Remove and reserve.

Julienne apples with a mandoline. Add parsley and enough vinaigrette to moisten apples.

In a bowl, combine all ingredients and reserve at room temperature.

Place escalopes in a very hot skillet and sear again for 2 or 3 minutes on each side.

Add a pinch of fleur de sel before serving.

Vin de glace Gewürztraminer
Vignoble de la Chapelle Ste-Agnès

See Bontés Divines page 21
See Verger Le Gros Pierre page 125

Flavours of a Region *Eastern Townships*

Flavours of a Region *Eastern Townships*

LEG OF GOAT FROM CHÈVRERIE FRUIT D'UNE PASSION
POLENTA AND ROASTED RED PEPPERS

Pour oil into a heavy cooking pot and sear leg of goat on all sides. Season with salt, pepper, and paprika. Remove the meat and reduce heat. Add onions and glaze well. Add garlic and rosemary. Deglaze with wine.

Moisten with veal stock. Add bay leaves, lovage, and cloves. Return meat to the pot and cover. Cook in a pre-heated 190°C (375°F) oven for approximately 2 hours, turning and basting occasionally.

Serves 4

1	1.5 kg (3 lb 4 oz) leg of goat	
30 mL	olive oil	2 tablespoons
3	onions, finely chopped	
5	cloves garlic, minced	
2	sprigs fresh rosemary	
200 mL	rosé wine	3/4 cup
1 L	veal stock	4 cups
3	bay leaves	
2	stalks lovage	
2	cloves	
	salt, pepper, paprika	

In a bowl, moisten pieces of red pepper with olive oil. Add salt, pepper, and paprika. Cook in a skillet until tender. Reserve warm.

Roasted red peppers

3	small red peppers, seeded and cut in 4	
45 mL	olive oil	3 tablespoons
	salt, pepper, paprika	

Pour oil into a saucepan and sweat onion and garlic. Moisten with broth and bring to a boil. Season and add bay leaf.

Slowly add polenta and mix well. Cook at medium heat for 5 minutes, stirring constantly. Remove from heat and let stand 10 minutes without stirring. Remove bay leaf and adjust seasoning. Blend in the cheese.

Pour the polenta into an ovenproof dish and cool in the refrigerator. Cut individual portions and warm in the oven with a little butter.

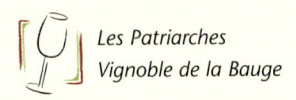

Polenta

30 mL	onion, minced	2 tablespoons
1	clove garlic, minced	
25 mL	olive oil	5 teaspoons
500 mL	poultry broth	2 cups
1	bay leaf	
250 mL	polenta	1 cup
30 mL	parmesan, grated	2 tablespoons
	salt and pepper	

Les Patriarches
Vignoble de la Bauge

See Chèvrerie Fruit d'une Passion page 24

LOIN OF CERF DE HIGHWATER
CRANBERRY CHUTNEY

Serves 4

1	170 g (6 oz) deer loin	
5 mL	sea salt	1 teaspoon
2.5 mL	ground black peppercorns	1/2 teaspoon
2.5 mL	ground pink peppercorns	1/2 teaspoon
1.25 mL	ground nutmeg	1/4 teaspoon
1.25 mL	ground cumin	1/4 teaspoon
185 mL	red wine	3/4 cup
30 mL	olive oil	2 tablespoons
15 mL	butter	1 tablespoon

Cranberry chutney

250 mL	fresh cranberries	1 cup
1	medium onion, thinly sliced	
15 mL	olive oil	1 tablespoon
125 mL	balsamic vinegar	1/2 cup
60 mL	red wine	1/4 cup
30 mL	white sugar	2 tablespoons
5 mL	chopped fresh ginger	1 teaspoon
	salt and pepper	

Combine spices and coat meat generously.

Heat olive oil and butter in an ovenproof skillet. Sear meat on all sides.

Place skillet in a preheated 200°C (400°F) oven and cook for 10 minutes. Turn meat and cook for another 10 minutes. Remove meat from skillet and let stand for 10 minutes. In the same skillet, reduce wine by half. Strain. Reserve warm.

In a skillet, sweat onions and ginger in olive oil.

Combine remaining ingredients. Cover, reduce heat, and simmer until liquid has evaporated.

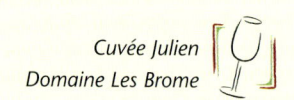

Cuvée Julien
Domaine Les Brome

See Ferme de Cerfs Highwater page 123

Flavours of a Region *Eastern Townships*

Flavours of a Region *Eastern Townships*

BISON EN PORTEFEUILLE FROM DOMAINE DU BISON
VEGETABLES AND TOMME DES JOYEUX FROMAGERS FROM CHÈVRERIE FRUIT D'UNE PASSION

Heat butter and oil in a skillet and sauté vegetables. Season and reserve.

Spread equal portions of sautéed vegetables and cheese on the escalopes. Roll and tie up securely. Sear on all sides in the skillet, then place in a dripping pan. Cook in a preheated 190°C (375°F) oven for 5 minutes.

Pour the wine into a saucepan. Reduce by half. Add shallots and reduce by a quarter.

Add demi-glace and reduce to desired consistency.

Serves 4

4	125 g (4 1/2 oz) escalopes of bison	
15 mL	butter	1 tablespoon
15 mL	olive oil	1 tablespoon
1	red pepper, seeded and finely diced	
3	shallots, chopped	
1	clove garlic, finely chopped	
1	zucchini, finely diced	
120 g	cheese, thinly sliced	4 ounces
	salt and pepper	

Red wine sauce

250 mL	red wine	1 cup
2	shallots, chopped	
200 mL	demi-glace	3/4 cup

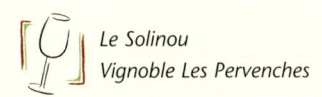

Le Solinou
Vignoble Les Pervenches

See Domaine du Bison page 123
See Chèvrerie Fruit d'une Passion page 24

Flavours of a Region *Eastern Townships*

ROCK CORNISH HEN
WITH RED PEPPER JELLY IN COARSE SALT CRUST

In a skillet, melt butter with olive oil and sear hens on both sides of the breast. Coat hens entirely with red pepper jelly. Season with pepper.

Do not salt the hens.

Combine all the ingredients in a bowl. Using a rolling pin, roll out half of the dough to a thickness of 5 mm (1/4 in). Cut out two ovals slightly larger than the size of the hens and place one hen on each rolled-out sheet of dough.

Divide the remaining dough into two equal parts. Roll out and cover the hens, sealing the two sheets of dough together. If the dough breaks, patch it with small pieces, smoothing the surface with your fingers and a little water. Brush with the glaze and cook in a preheated 180°C (350°F) oven for approximately 40 minutes.

When ready to serve, break the dough and remove the hens.

Do not eat the dough.

Serves 4

2	whole Rock Cornish hens	
90 mL	red pepper jelly	6 tablespoons
15 mL	butter	1 tablespoon
15 mL	olive oil	1 tablespoon
	pepper	

Coarse salt dough

500 mL	coarse salt	2 cups
650 mL	flour	2 5/8 cups
4	egg whites	
200 mL	water	3/4 cup
1.25 mL	dry thyme or rosemary	1/4 teaspoon
	glaze (egg + water)	

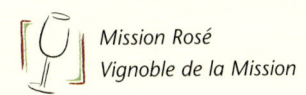

Mission Rosé
Vignoble de la Mission

ROULÉ OF LAPIN DE STANSTEAD AND APPLES FROM VERGER LE GROS PIERRE

Serves 4

1	1.5 kg (3 lb 4 oz) whole rabbit, boned	
1	apple, peeled and cut in wedges	
1.25 mL	garlic flower	1/4 teaspoon
45 mL	Dijon mustard	3 tablespoons
30 mL	thyme	2 tablespoons
	salt and pepper	

Tarragon sauce

1	medium onion, finely chopped	
5 mL	garlic flower	1 teaspoon
1 bunch	fresh tarragon	
250 mL	white wine	1 cup
15 mL	cider vinegar	1 tablespoon
1 L	poultry stock	4 cups
500 mL	35% cream	2 cups
	salt and pepper	

In a bowl, combine apple, garlic flower, salt, and pepper. Spread this preparation over the boned rabbit. Roll up and tie securely.

Place the meat on a skewer and brush with mustard. Sprinkle with thyme and cook on the barbecue at low heat or in a dripping pan in a preheated 180°C (350 °F) oven for 40 minutes.

Remove the skewer and wrap the meat in tinfoil. Reserve for approximately 15 minutes. Remove the string and cut into 8 slices.

In a saucepan, combine onion, garlic, and half the tarragon leaves. Moisten with white wine. Season. Bring to a boil and reduce until almost dry. Add vinegar and boil for 1 minute. Pour in poultry stock and cream. Reduce until sauce thickens. Purée in a blender, then strain through a chinois. Season and add remaining tarragon leaves. Reheat before serving.

La Vieille Grange
Vignoble Les Blancs Côteaux

See Lapins de Stanstead page 123
See Verger Le Gros Pierre page 125

Flavours of a Region *Eastern Townships*

BOBINES TROUT WITH PART DES ANGES FROM L'ORPAILLEUR
ABBAYE DE SAINT-BENOÎT GRUYÈRE PILLOW

Serves 4

4	160 g (5 1/2 oz) trout filets	
30 mL	olive oil	2 tablespoons
90 mL	Part des Anges	6 tablespoons
250 mL	red peppers, julienned*	1 cup
185 mL	15% country cream	3/4 cup
	pepper	
	fleur de sel	

Gruyère pillow

250 mL	long grain rice	1 cup
30 mL	olive oil	2 tablespoons
45 mL	red onion, chopped	3 tablespoons
500 mL	poultry broth	2 cups
1	bay leaf	
1.25 mL	fresh thyme	1/4 teaspoon
160 mL	red, yellow, and green peppers, finely diced	2/3 cup
150 g	grated gruyère cheese	5 1/2 ounces
	salt and pepper	

Remove skin and fat from filets and cut in three pieces. Heat olive oil in a skillet and sauté filets for 1 minute on each side. Deglaze with Part des Anges.

Remove filets and reserve. Add the julienned pepper and cream and reduce by half. Season with pepper.

* *Reserve one quarter of the julienned peppers in ice water to use later as garnish.*

Heat olive oil in a saucepan and brown rice with onions.

Moisten with stock. Add bay leaf and thyme. Bring to a boil and cook in a preheated 180°C (350°F) oven for 12 minutes.

Add peppers and cheese. Combine well. Season. Divide equally into ramekins. Cook in a preheated 180°C (350°F) oven for 15 minutes. Reserve.

Place the filets on the cheese pillow, alternating with the julienned peppers. Add a pinch of fleur de sel before serving.

L'Orpailleur élevé en fût de chêne
Vignoble de l'Orpailleur

See Ferme Piscicole des Bobines page 123
See Vignoble de l'Orpailleur page 15
See Abbaye de Saint-Benoît-du-Lac page 123

Flavours of a Region *Eastern Townships*

93

Flavours of a Region *Eastern Townships*

Desserts

BALUCHON OF BLEU ERMITE FROM ABBAYE DE SAINT-BENOÎT
SAUTÉED PEARS AND BALSAMIC VINEGAR REDUCTION
Steven Beyrouty – *Auberge Georgeville 1889*

LAC-MÉGANTIC WILD BLUEBERRY BAVAROIS
James Stearns – *Auberge Les Victorines du Lac*

LAVENDER CRÈME BRÛLÉE
FROM BLEU LAVANDE AND BEURRERIE DU PATRIMOINE
François Dubois – *Le Bocage*

ICE CREAM FROM LAITERIE DE COATICOOK
AND ACCOMPANIMENTS
Dominic Tremblay – *Café Massawippi*

FIELD STRAWBERRY AND LEMON BALM GRANITÉ
Steven Beyrouty – *Auberge Georgeville 1889*

BLUEBERRY FLOATING ISLANDS FROM COLLINE AUX BLEUETS
Stéphane Charpentier – *Auberge West Brome*

BERRIES FROM BLEUETIÈRE MI-VALLON
AND CHIBOUSTE AU GRATIN
Roland Ménard – *Hovey Manor*

APPLE TARTLETS AND MAPLE CARAMEL
Hans Christiner – *Auberge du Joli Vent*

Flavours of a Region *Eastern Townships*

BALUCHON OF BLEU ERMITE FROM ABBAYE DE SAINT-BENOÎT
SAUTEED PEARS AND BALSAMIC VINEGAR REDUCTION

Combine the first four ingredients and purée in food processor. Season.

Using a pastry brush, brush 4 sheets of phyllo pastry measuring 12.5 cm x 12.5 cm (5 in x 5 in) with olive oil. Repeat four times. Divide the cheese mixture into four equal portions and place one portion in the centre of each sheet. Bring the corners of pastry together to form a monk's bag. Bake in a preheated 180°C (350°F) oven for 10 minutes. Reserve warm.

In a saucepan, reduce balsamic vinegar by half.

In a hot skillet, sweat onions in oil. Add remaining ingredients. Stir over medium heat for 5 minutes. Reserve warm.

Serves 4

120 g	blue cheese	4 ounces
15 mL	pistachios (shelled)	1 tablespoon
15 mL	chopped dry shallots	1 tablespoon
60 mL	dry white wine	1/4 cup
16 sheets	phyllo pastry	
45 mL	olive oil	3 tablespoons
	salt and black pepper	

125 mL	balsamic vinegar	1/2 cup

Sautéed pears

2	pears, halved, cored, and thinly sliced	
1	medium onion, halved and thinly sliced	
30 mL	olive oil	2 tablespoons
60 mL	rice wine	1/4 cup
5 mL	brown sugar	1 teaspoon
	salt and black pepper	

Vendange Tardive
Vignoble La Mission

See Abbaye de Saint-Benoît-du-Lac page 123

LAC-MÉGANTIC WILD BLUEBERRY BAVAROIS

Serves 4

200 mL	wild blueberry coulis	3/4 cup
1 pouch	unflavoured gelatine	
	juice of 1 lemon	
200 mL	35% cream	3/4 cup

In a large cul-de-poule, spinkle gelatine over lemon juice. Reserve for 5 minutes.

Whip cream until it thickens. Reserve.

Place cul-de-poule over a saucepan filled with boiling water to melt gelatine.

Whisk in the coulis, then gently fold in the whipped cream. Pour the mixture into moulds and cool in the refrigerator for at least 2 hours.

Vin de glace Givrée d'Ardois Rosé
Domaine des Côtes d'Ardoise

Flavours of a Region *Eastern Townships*

Flavours of a Region *Eastern Townships*

LAVENDER CRÈME BRÛLÉE FROM BLEU LAVANDE
AND BEURRERIE DU PATRIMOINE

In a saucepan, heat cream with lavender over low heat. Steep for 15 minutes and remove lavender.

In a bowl, beat egg yolks. Sprinkle the sugar-cornstarch mixture into the eggs. Add honey in a thin trickle, and beat until egg yolks are light and frothy.

Pour hot cream over the egg yolk mixture, stirring well. Pour into the saucepan and stir constantly over very low heat until the cream coats the back of a wooden spoon. Place saucepan in a bath of ice to stop it from cooking.

Pour the mixture into cored apples and cool in the refrigerator for at least 4 hours. When ready to serve, sprinkle sugar on top and brown with a blowtorch or a crème brûlée iron. Let stand until the sugar hardens.

Serves 4

4	large apples, cored	
500 mL	45% cream	2 cups
2 sprigs	lavender	
5	egg yolks	
60 mL	sugar + some to sprinkle combined with	1/4 cup
2.5 mL	cornstarch	1/2 teaspoon
60 mL	hot liquid honey	1/4 cup

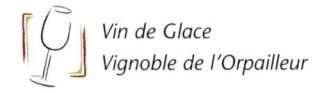

Vin de Glace
Vignoble de l'Orpailleur

See Beurrerie du Patrimoine page 18
See Bleu Lavande page 28

ICE CREAM FROM LAITERIE DE COATICOOK
AND ACCOMPANIMENTS

Serves 4

Vanilla ice cream and pear milkshake

30 mL	sugar	2 tablespoons
1	pear, thinly sliced	
125 mL	35% cream	1/2 cup
125 mL	milk	1/2 cup
1 pod	vanilla, seeded	
	foamed milk	

In a non-stick skillet, caramelize sugar until golden. Add pear and sauté for a few seconds. Add cream, milk, and vanilla. Bring to a boil. Purée in a blender, then strain through a chinois. Cool in the refrigerator.

Maple taffy ice cream and maple soufflé

4	egg whites	
125 mL	confectioner's sugar	1/2 cup
125 mL	maple syrup	1/2 cup
15 mL	maple liqueur	1 tablespoon
15 mL	baking powder	1 tablespoon
pinch	salt	

Using an eggbeater, beat eggs in a bowl until firm. Mix in sugar and baking powder gradually. Pour in the maple syrup and liqueur, beating until the mixture is smooth.

Fill small ramekins halfway and bake in a 190°C (375°F) oven for 6 to 8 minutes. The soufflé will double in volume.

Strawberry ice cream, shortbread, and sour strawberry compote

4	shortbread cookies	
8	large strawberries, quartered	
60 mL	sugar	1/4 cup
	zest of 1 lemon	
	juice of 1 lemon	
5 mL	raspberry vinegar	1 teaspoon

In a bowl, combine strawberries, zest, and sugar.

Pour the mixture into a hot, non-stick skillet and heat until the fruit is stewed. Add lemon juice and raspberry vinegar. Cool in the refrigerator.

Vin de Glace
Vignoble La Mission

See Laiterie de Coaticook page 30

Flavours of a Region *Eastern Townships*

Flavours of a Region *Eastern Townships*

FIELD STRAWBERRY AND LEMON BALM GRANITÉ

Serves 4

500 mL	fresh strawberries	2 cups
100 mL	cranberry juice	3/8 cup
1/2	bunch fresh lemon balm, coarsely chopped	
15 mL	lemon juice	1 tablespoon
125 mL	white sugar	1/2 cup

Place chopped lemon balm in a large non-reactive bowl. Combine all the ingredients in a blender, except the lemon balm.

Simmer the mixture in a covered saucepan over medium heat for 15 minutes. Remove from heat and pour into a bowl over the lemon balm. Cover with plastic wrap and let steep for 15 minutes.

Strain through a chinois and pour into a plastic container. When cool, cover the purée with plastic wrap and freeze for 24 hours.

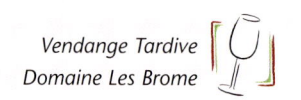

Vendange Tardive
Domaine Les Brome

Flavours of a Region *Eastern Townships*

BLUEBERRY FLOATING ISLANDS
FROM COLLINE AUX BLEUETS

Serves 4

500 mL	blueberries	2 cups
10 mL	water	2 teaspoons
125 mL	sugar	1/2 cup
	juice of 1 lemon	
250 mL	egg whites	1 cup
280 mL	caster sugar	1 cup + 2 tablespoons
	a few drops of vanilla extract	
pinch	salt	
100 g	slivered almonds	3 1/2 ounces

Pour water, blueberries, sugar, and lemon juice into a saucepan and simmer for 20 minutes.

Using an egg beater, beat eggs in a bowl until firm. Add sugar, vanilla extract, and salt. Spoon into a piping bag with a fluted socket.

Line a cookie sheet with non-stick paper and create 4 large meringue islands. Sprinkle with almonds. Bake in a preheated 230°C (450°F) oven for approximately 1 1/2 to 2 minutes.

Vendange Tardive Bise d'Automne
Domaine du Ridge

See Colline aux Bleuets page 123

Flavours of a Region *Eastern Townships*

BERRIES FROM BLEUETIÈRE MI-VALLON
AND CHIBOUSTE AU GRATIN

Serves 6

750 mL	blueberries	3 cups

Meringue*

250 mL	sugar	1 cup
6	egg whites	

Chiboust cream

160 mL	whole milk	2/3 cup
160 mL	35% cream	2/3 cup
60 mL	sugar	1/4 cup
30 mL	cornstarch	2 tablespoons
6	egg yolks	
1	pouch unflavoured gelatine	
45 mL	water	3 tablespoons
1/2 pod	vanilla	

In a bowl, beat eggs with an eggbeater until they form firm peaks. Gradually add sugar while beating. Reserve.

* Prepare meringue first.

Prepare the gelatine in a small bowl, following the manufacturer's instructions. Reserve.

Using a sharp knife, cut the vanilla pod lengthwise and scrape out the seeds.

In a saucepan, bring milk, cream, and vanilla to a simmer over low heat. In a bowl, whisk sugar and cornstarch into the egg yolks until smooth. Pour the mixture into the saucepan, stirring constantly.

Bring to a boil and simmer for 3 to 4 minutes, until the mixture thickens. Remove the saucepan from the heat. Stirring constantly, mix in the gelatine and then fold in the meringue.

Preheat the oven to its highest setting.

Pour equal portions of blueberries into ramekins and top generously with chiboust cream. Place ramekins in the oven and broil for approximately 3 minutes or until the top of the chiboust cream begins to brown.

Vin de Glace Cuvée Nadège
Vignoble Les Trois Clochers

See Bleuetière Mi-Vallon page 123

Flavours of a Region *Eastern Townships*

APPLE TARTLETS AND MAPLE CARAMEL

Serves 4

| 600 g | sweet pastry dough | 1 pound 5 ounces |

Maple caramel

| 150 mL | 35% cream | 5/8 cup |
| 150 mL | medium maple syrup | 5/8 cup |

Apple filling

2	Cortland apples, peeled and finely diced	
125 mL	apple juice	1/2 cup
2	egg yolks	

With a rolling pin, roll out the dough and cut rolled-out pastries to line 4 tart moulds measuring 12 cm (4 3/4 in) in diameter. Bake in a preheated 180°C (350°F) oven until the crust begins to brown. Reserve.

Heat cream and syrup in a saucepan, stirring constantly. Reduce by two-thirds. Cool to room temperature. Reserve.

In a saucepan, cook apples in apple juice over low heat (they should remain firm). Remove the apples and cool. Reserve the juice.

In a bowl, mix egg yolks with maple caramel and apple juice.

Place apples in pie crust and pour caramel over the apples. Bake in a preheated 150°C (300°F) oven for approximately 20 minutes.

Cidre de Glace
Domaine Pinnacle

Flavours of a Region *Eastern Townships*

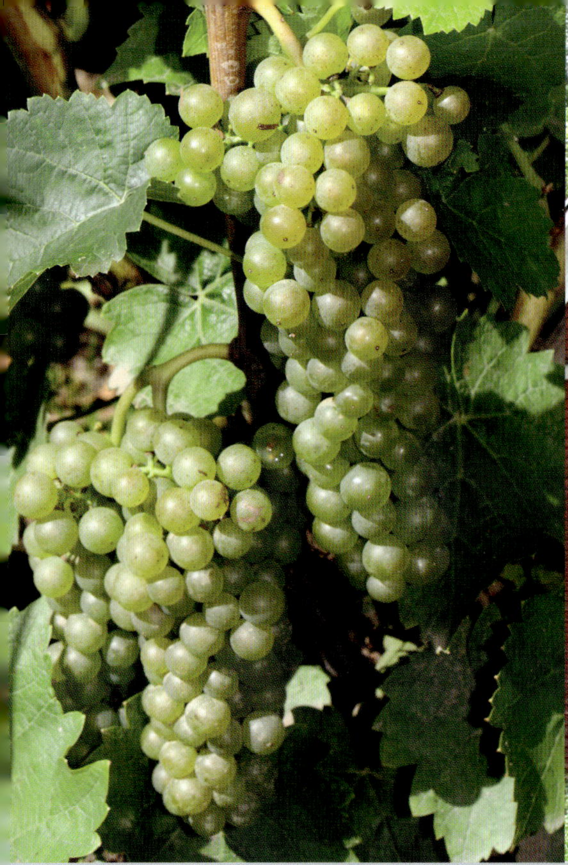
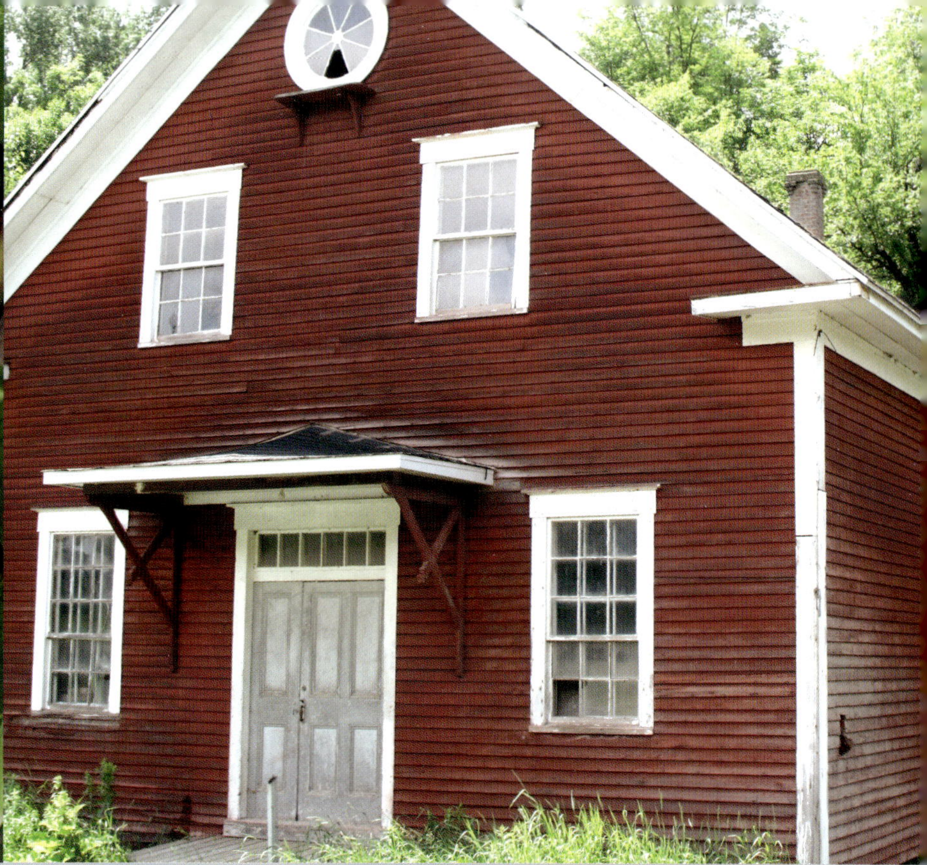
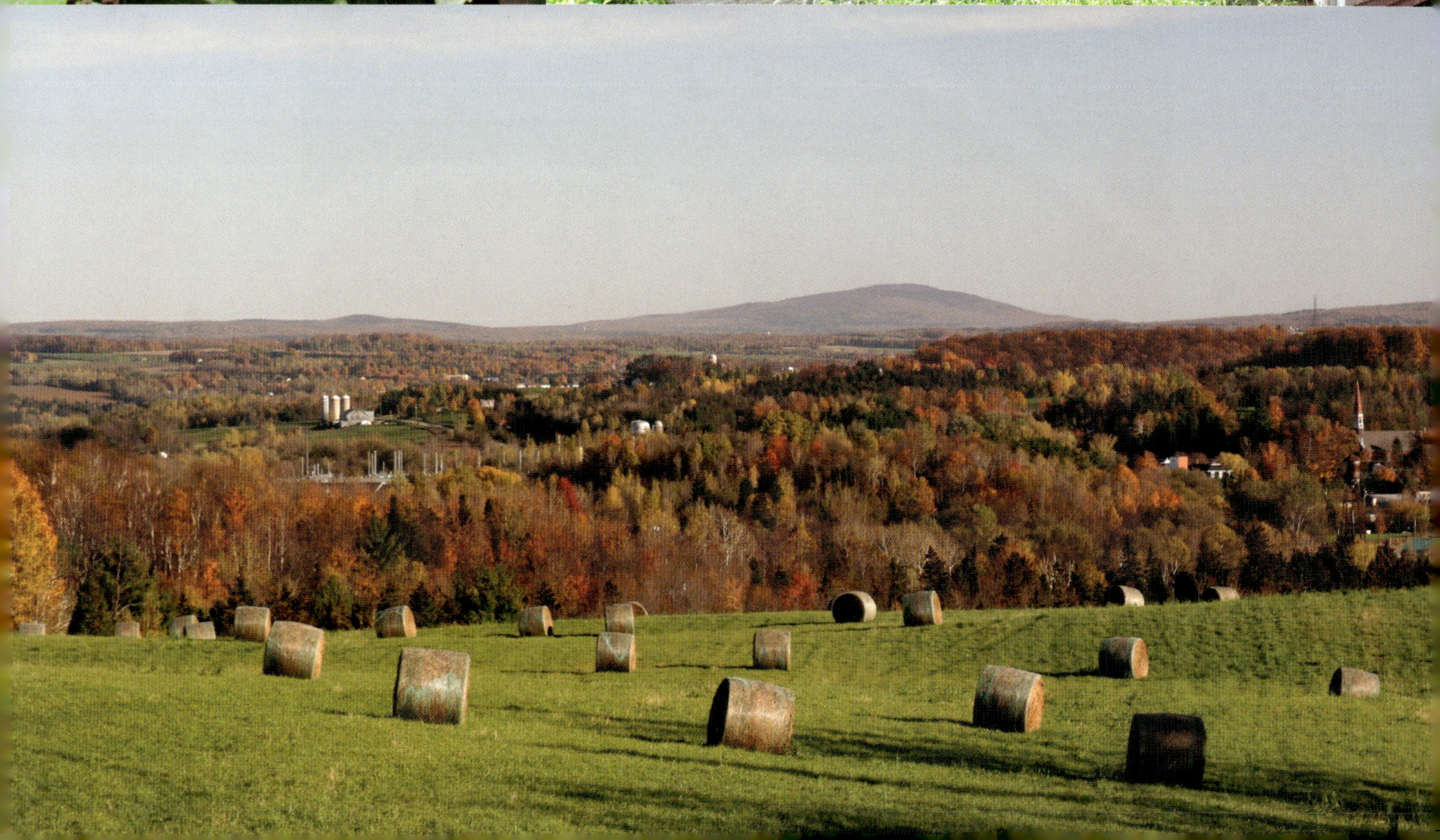

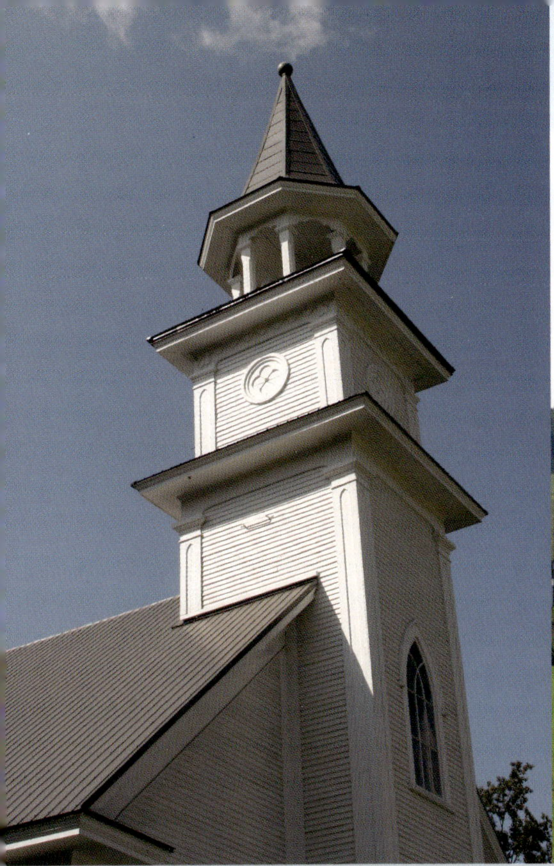
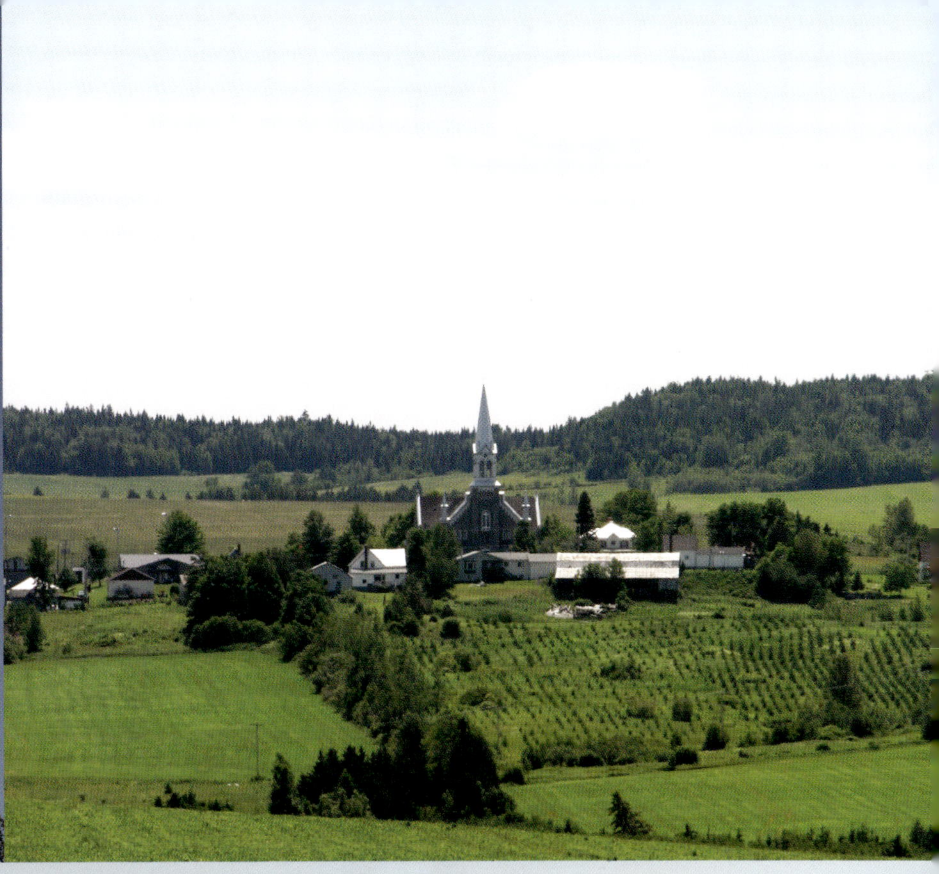
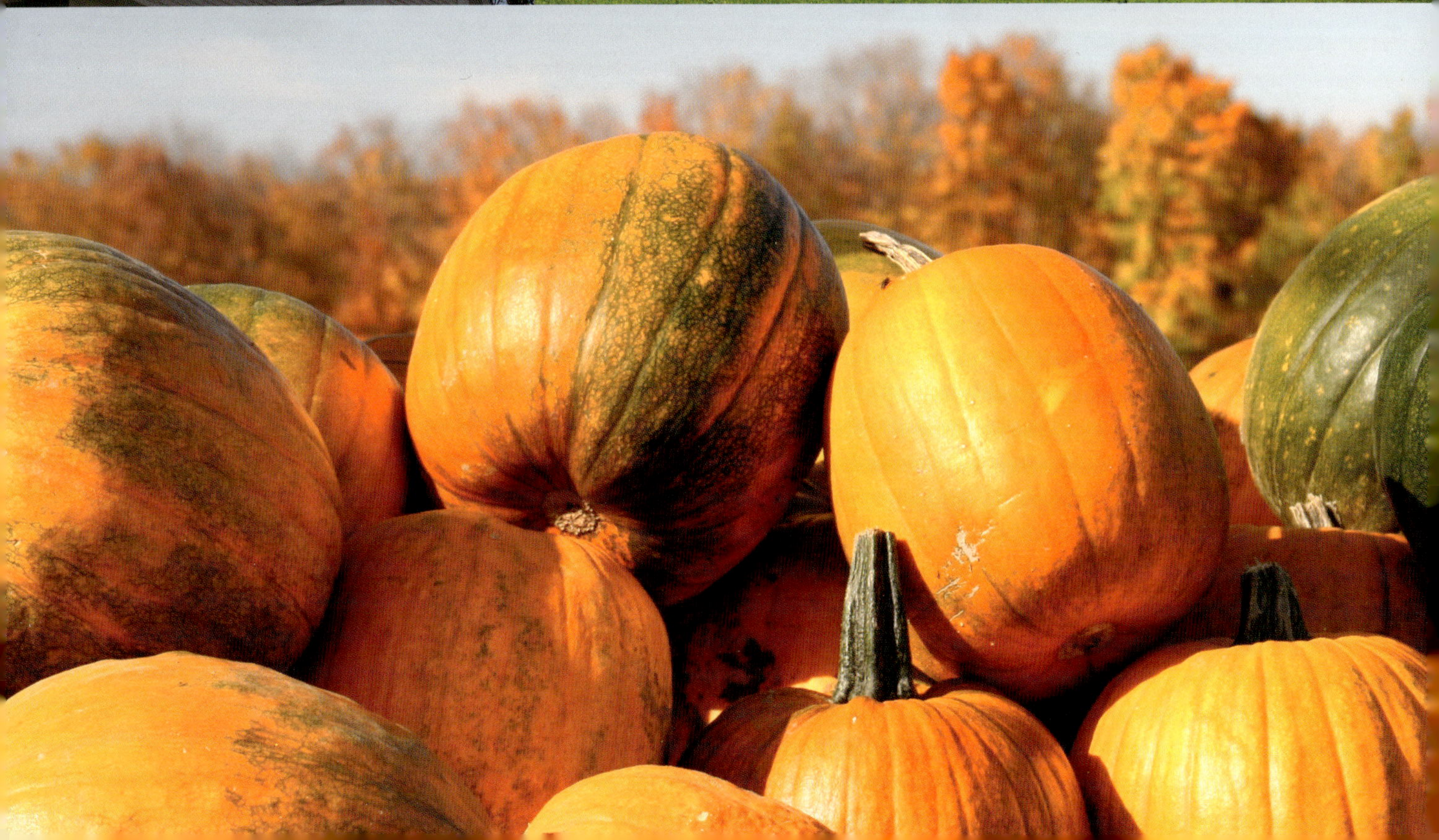

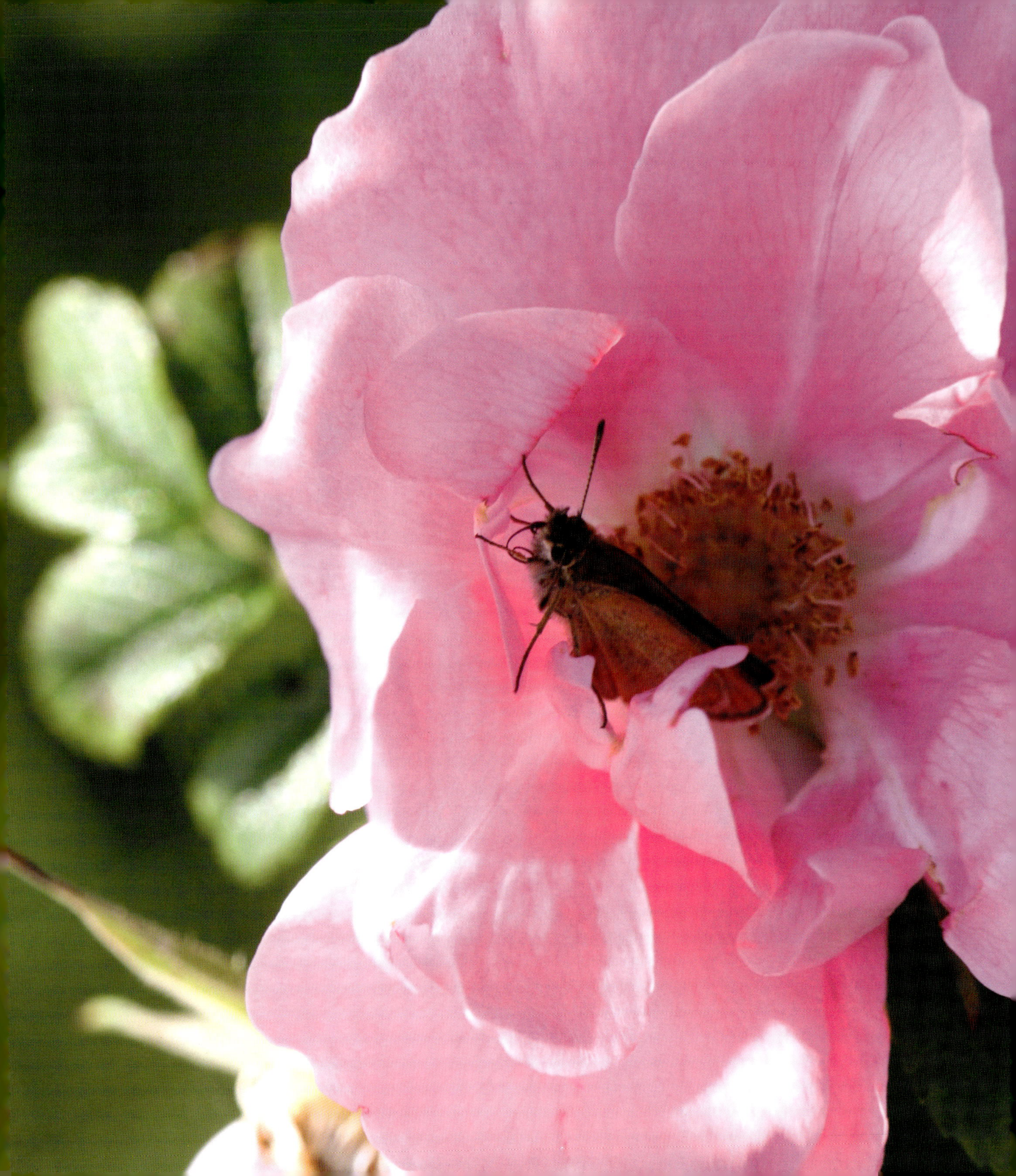

My thanks go out to:

... all the artisans, producers, vine and apple growers, chefs, and innkeepers. Your wisdom and know-how are immensely enriching;

... to Jacques Proulx, president and founder of Solidarité rurale du Québec, for sharing his knowledge and convictions. Thanks to his contribution, we are better equipped to understand the commitment made by every generation of people living in our rural regions;

... to Danie Béliveau and Alain Larouche from the Eastern Townships Tourism Association, for their encouragement and for sharing in my enthusiasm;

... to Julie Sage from CLD de la MRC de Coaticook, for helping me discover the prettiest views as well as a multitude of other, more secret places in the region;

... to Philippe Lapeyrie, sommelier, for his suggestions in wine pairing;

... to Vera Roy for her keen eye revising texts;

... to Christiane Caya, for her support since the very beginning;

... and to all my friends and readers, thank you for your encouragement!

Provence?

EASTERN TOWNSHIPS!

50 packages for vacation ideas on
www.easterntownships.org

RECIPES INDEX

Soups

	Page
CREAM OF SQUASH AND BRISE DU VIGNERON FROM FROMAGERIE DES CANTONS *Stéphane Charpentier – Auberge West Brome*	50
YELLOW TOMATO GAZPACHO FROM SANDERS FARM *Roland Ménard – Hovey Manor*	52
POTAGE EN DUO BEET FROM VALLONS MARAÎCHERS AND APPLE FROM VERGER LE GROS PIERRE *François Dubois – Le Bocage*	54
VELOUTÉ OF ASPARAGUS *James Stearns – Auberge Les Victorines du Lac*	56

Appetizers

	Page
BRAISED PORK JOWLS AGNOLOTTI WITH MOÛT DE P.O.M. BOUDIN NOIR À LA NORMANDE *Roland Ménard – Hovey Manor*	60
CAPRICE DES CANTONS FROM FROMAGERIE LA GERMAINE LAVENDER FROM BLEU LAVANDE AND HONEY FONDANT *Dominic Tremblay – Café Massawippi*	62
FIDDLEHEAD FLAN FROM PRODUITS INDIGÈNES GOAT CHEESE TUILE *Martine Satre – Le temps des cerises*	64
DUCK PASTILLA FROM BONTÉS DIVINES CRANBERRY CHUTNEY *Martine Satre – Le temps des cerises*	66
POACHED PEAR, DUCK FOIE GRAS FROM BONTÉS DIVINES LAKE BROME DUCK LIVERS AND ARCHER FROM CEP D'ARGENT *Jacques Poulain – Château Bromont*	68
PRESSÉ OF RABBIT FROM LAPINS DE STANSTEAD AND DUCK FOIE GRAS FROM DUCS DE MONTRICHARD *Alain Labrie – Groupe Germain*	70
SWISS CHARD SPÄTZLI AND TOMME DES JOYEUX FROMAGERS GRATIN FROM CHÈVRERIE FRUIT D'UNE PASSION *Hans Christiner – Auberge du Joli Vent*	72

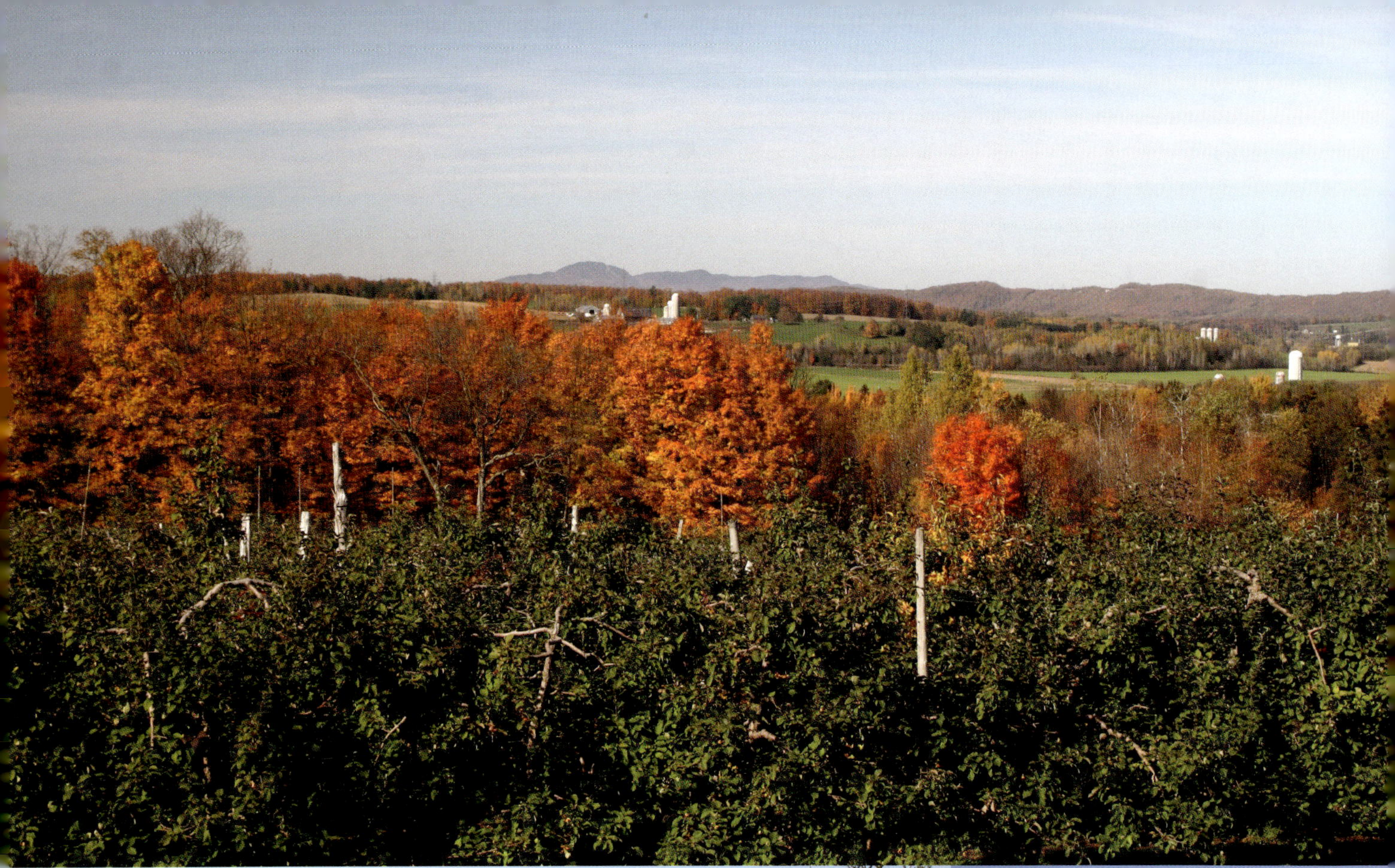

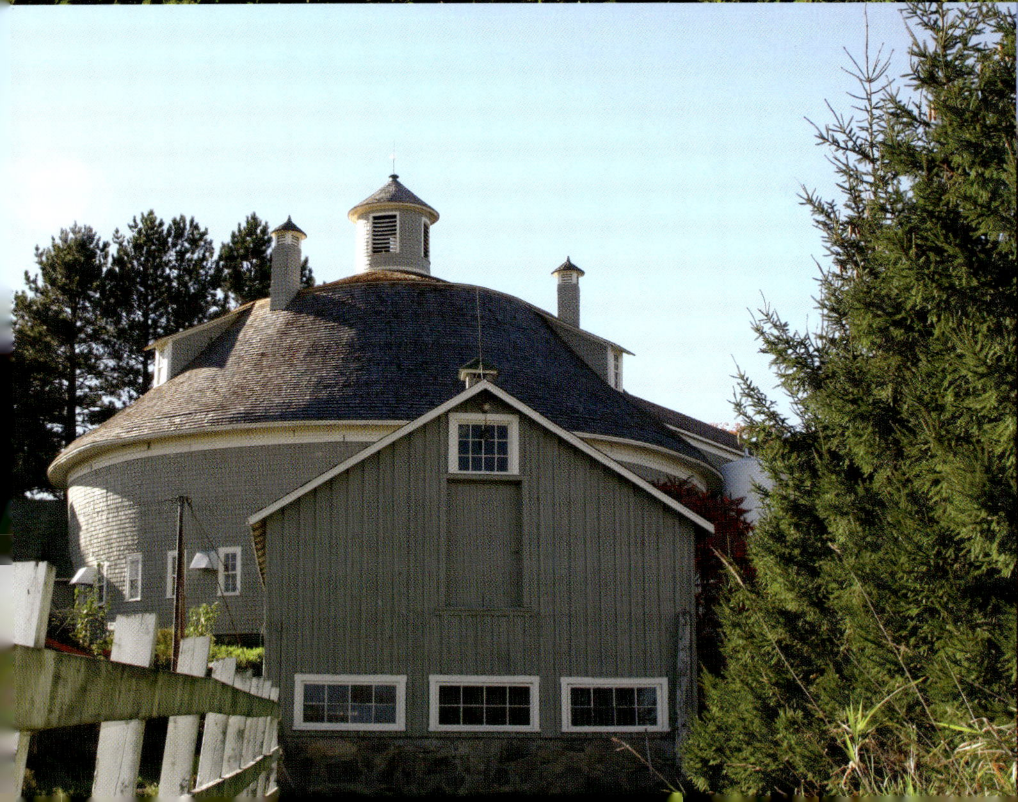

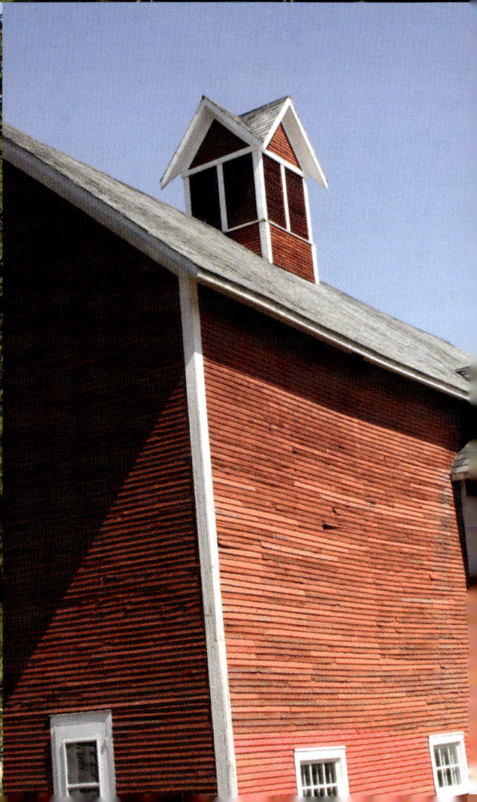

RECIPES INDEX (CONT.)

Page   *Page*

Main Dishes

BRAISED LAMB FROM FERME MANASAN   76
Martine Satre – Le temps des cerises

RIB OF CERF DE HIGHWATER AND SHANK CONFIT   78
EGGPLANT AND ALFRED LE FERMIER GRATIN
FROM FROMAGERIE LA STATION
Alain Labrie – Groupe Germain

DUCK FOIE GRAS FROM BONTÉS DIVINES   80
APPLES FROM VERGER LE GROS PIERRE
Dominic Tremblay – Café Massawippi

LEG OF GOAT FROM   82
CHÈVRERIE FRUIT D'UNE PASSION
POLENTA AND ROASTED RED PEPPERS
Hans Christiner – Auberge du Joli Vent

LOIN OF CERF DE HIGHWATER   84
CRANBERRY CHUTNEY
Steven Beyrouty – Auberge Georgeville

BISON EN PORTEFEUILLE   86
FROM DOMAINE DU BISON
VEGETABLES AND TOMME
DES JOYEUX FROMAGERS
FROM CHÈVRERIE FRUIT D'UNE PASSION
James Stearns – Auberge Les Victorines du Lac

ROCK CORNISH HEN WITH   88
RED PEPPER JELLY IN COARSE SALT CRUST
Stéphane Charpentier – Auberge West Brome

ROULÉ OF LAPIN DE STANSTEAD   90
AND APPLES FROM VERGER LE GROS PIERRE
François Dubois – Le Bocage

BOBINES TROUT WITH   92
PART DES ANGES FROM L'ORPAILLEUR
ABBAYE DE SAINT-BENOÎT GRUYÈRE PILLOW
Jacques Poulain – Château Bromont

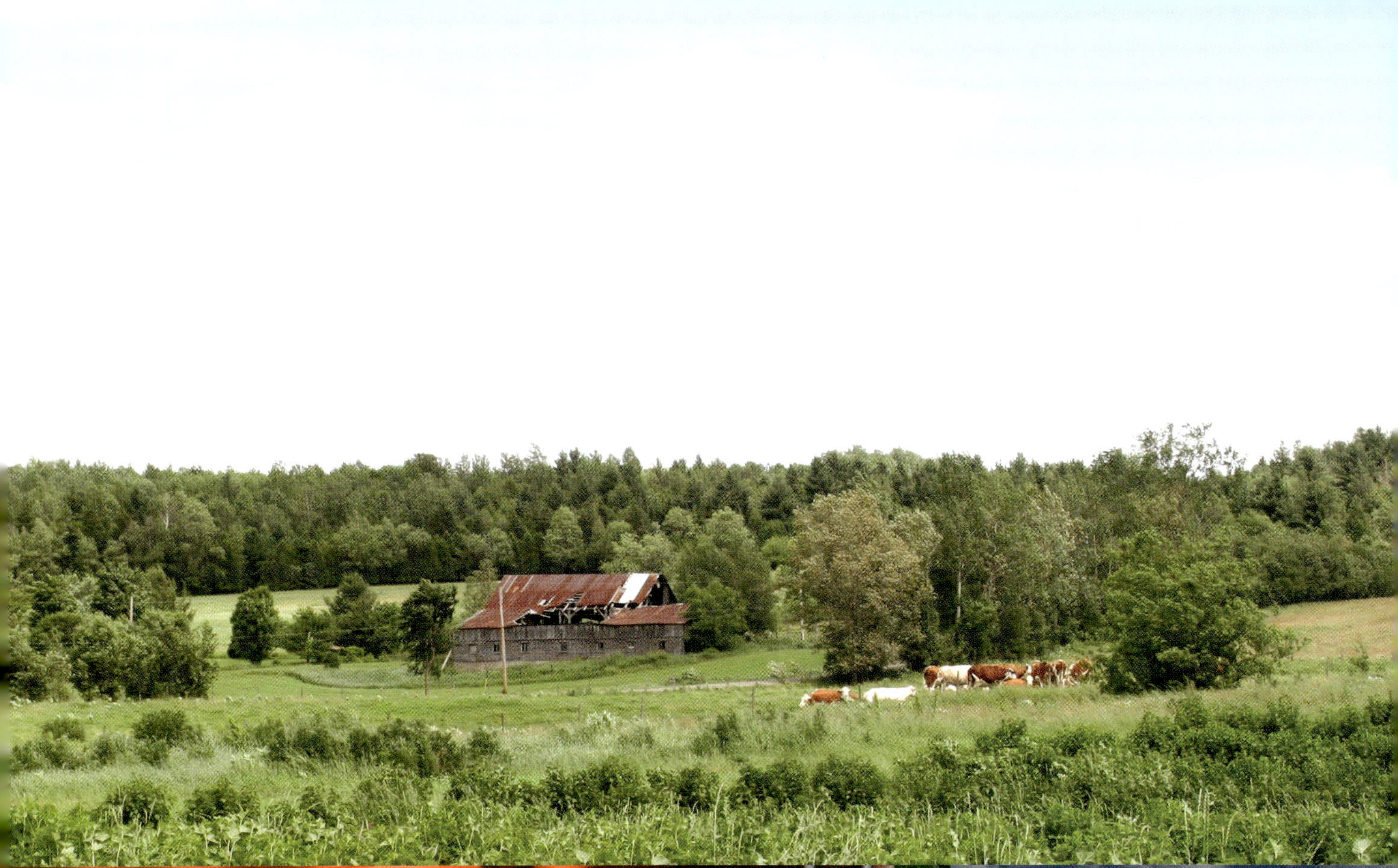

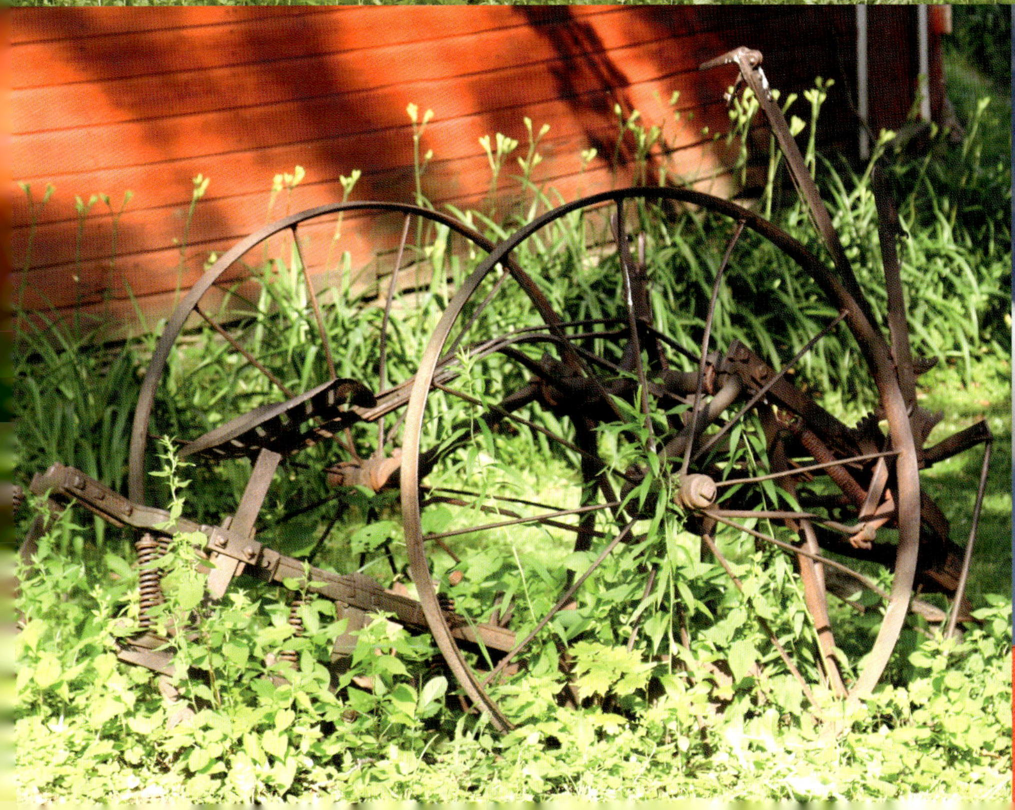

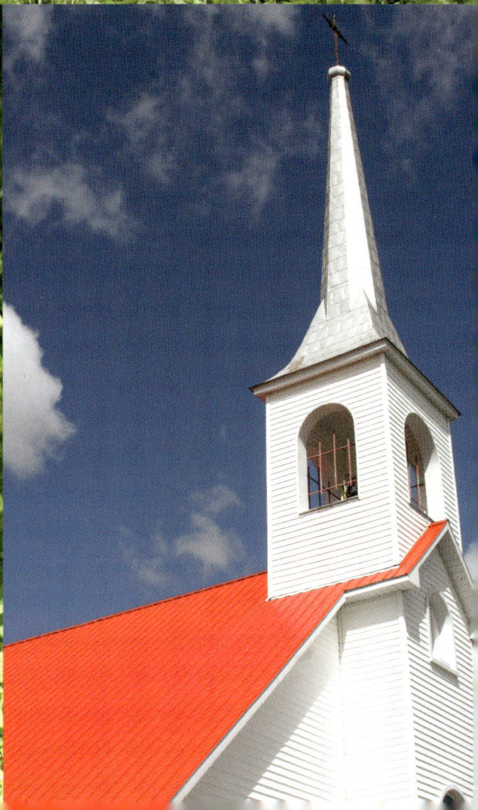

Flavours of a Region *Eastern Townships*

Recipes Index (cont.)

Page

Desserts

BALUCHON OF BLEU ERMITE FROM ABBAYE DE SAINT-BENOÎT SAUTÉED PEARS AND BALSAMIC VINEGAR REDUCTION *Steven Beyrouty – Auberge Georgeville*	96
LAC-MÉGANTIC WILD BLUEBERRY BAVAROIS *James Stearns – Auberge Les Victorines du Lac*	98
LAVENDER CRÈME BRÛLÉE FROM BLEU LAVANDE AND BEURRERIE DU PATRIMOINE *François Dubois – Le Bocage*	100
ICE CREAM FROM LAITERIE DE COATICOOK AND ACCOMPANIMENTS *Dominic Tremblay – Café Massawippi*	102
FIELD STRAWBERRY AND LEMON BALM GRANITÉ *Steven Beyrouty – Auberge Georgeville*	104
BLUEBERRY FLOATING ISLANDS FROM COLLINE AUX BLEUETS *Stéphane Charpentier – Auberge West Brome*	106
BERRIES FROM BLEUETIÈRE MI-VALLON AND CHIBOUSTE AU GRATIN *Roland Ménard – Hovey Manor*	108
APPLE TARTLETS AND MAPLE CARAMEL *Hans Christiner – Auberge du Joli Vent*	110

From our winter to your glass
Ice wine from Orpailleur vineyard

Vignoble de l'Orpailleur
Vine and wine ECONOMUSEUM
1086, route 202, Dunham (Québec), J0E 1M0
(450) 295-2763 www.orpailleur.ca
Restaurant Le Tire-Bouchon de l'Orpailleur
(450) 295-3335

Available in SAQ Code: 10220269

Gold medal
SÉLECTIONS MONDIALES DES VINS 2007

Best dessert Wine of the Year
ALL CANADIAN WINE CHAMPIONSHIPS 2006

★★★
★★
GOLD GRAPE
GUIDE MICHEL PHANEUF 2006

1873
de Milby

PRODUCERS

Abbaye de Saint-Benoît-du-Lac
1 rue Principale
Saint-Benoît-du-Lac
819-843-4336
1-877-343-4336
www.st-benoit-du-lac.com

Au cœur de la pomme
42 route 237
Frelighsburg
450-298-5319

Beurrerie du patrimoine
225 chemin Cochrane
Compton
819-835-9373
www.fermegroleau.com

Bleu Lavande
891 chemin Narrow
Fitch Bay
819-876-5851
www.bleulavande.ca

Bleuetière Mi-Vallon
375 chemin Flanders
Compton
819-835-9162

Bontés Divines (Les)
255 chemin Carrier
Stoke
819-878-3035
www.divinesbontes.com

Brome Lake Ducks
40 chemin du Centre
Knowlton
450-242-3825
www.canardsdulacbrome.com

**Chèvrerie Fruit
d'une passion (La)**
819-548-5705

Cidrerie Fleurs de pommiers
1047 route 202
Dunham
450-295-2223
www.fleursdepommiers.ca

Colline aux bleuets (La)
2259 chemin Beattie
Dunham
450-295-2417
www.collineauxbleuets.ca

Création Aline Crête
Magog
819-868-8878
www.crete-porcelaine.com

Domaine du Bison
27 rang Saint-Michel
Lambton
418-486-2652
www.domainedubison.com

Domaine des Travers du Roy
485 ave Centrale Sud (route 161)
Stratford
418-443-2020
www.traversduroy.com

Ducs de Montrichard
388 chemin Alfred-Desrochers
Orford
819-868-4217
www.ducsdemontrichard.com

Ferme de cerfs Highwater
52 chemin Rodrigue
Mansonville
450-292-4357 or 1-888-440-CERF
www.cerfhighwater.com

Ferme Manasan (La)
150 chemin Laberge
Danville
819-839-3350
www.manasan.qc.ca

Ferme Piscicole des Bobines
1 rue Saint-Henri
East Hereford
819-844-2418 or 1-800-819-2418
www.produitsdelaferme.com/bobines

Ferme Sanders
475 chemin Hyatt's Mills
Compton
819-849-2270
www.produitsdelaferme.com/sanders

Florasel
158 Miquelon
Saint-Camille
819-828-1224

Fromagerie des Cantons
441 boul. de Normandie Nord
Farnham
450-293-2498

Fromagerie La Germaine
819-849-3238

Fromagerie La Station
440 chemin Hatley
Compton
819-835-5301
www.fromagerielastation.com

Jardins du ruisseau Ball (Les)
Way's Mills
819-876-2210

Laiterie de Coaticook
1000 rue Child
Coaticook
819-849-2272 or 1-800-846-7224
www.laiteriedecoaticook.com

Lapins de Stanstead (Les)
819-876-7333
www.leslapinsdestanstead.ca

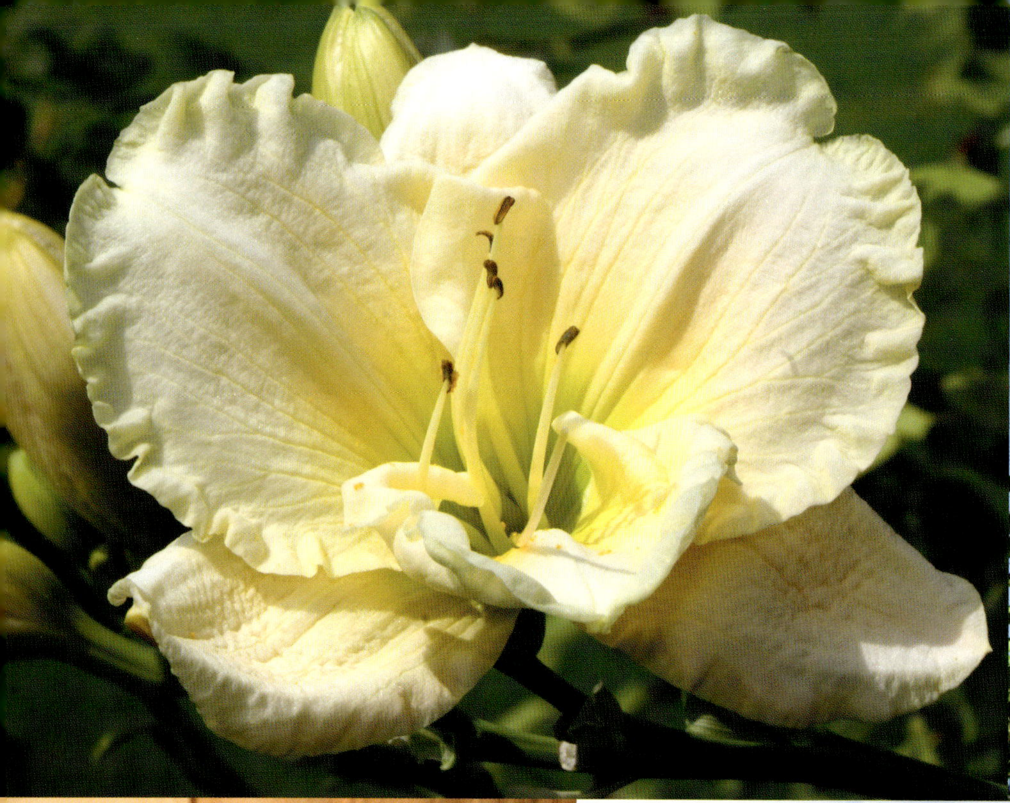

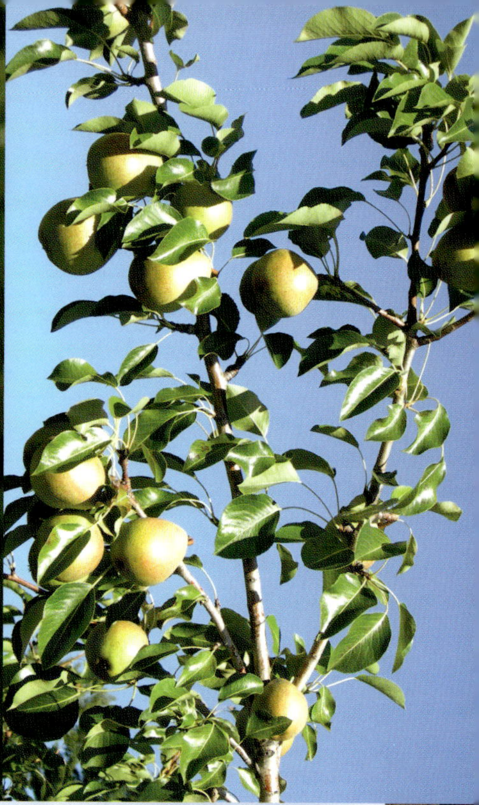

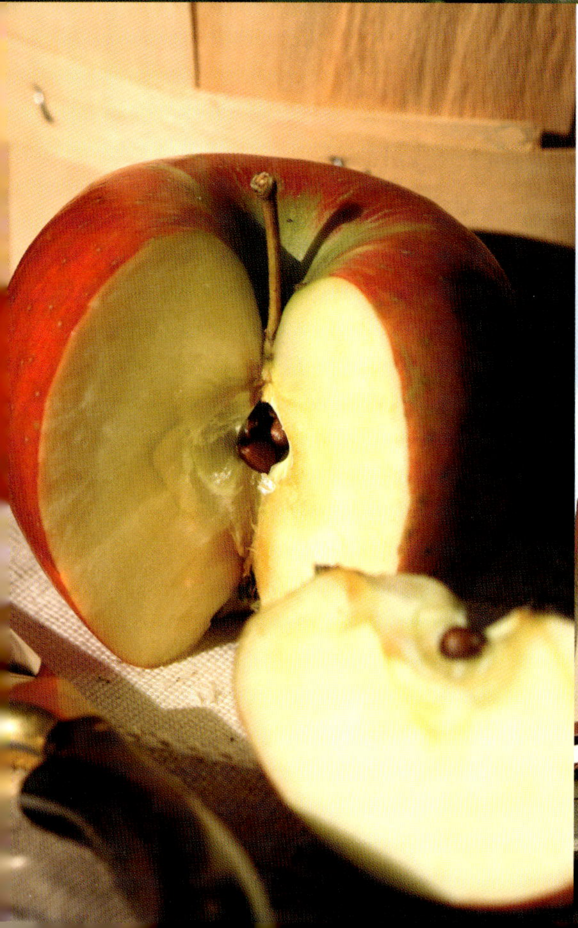

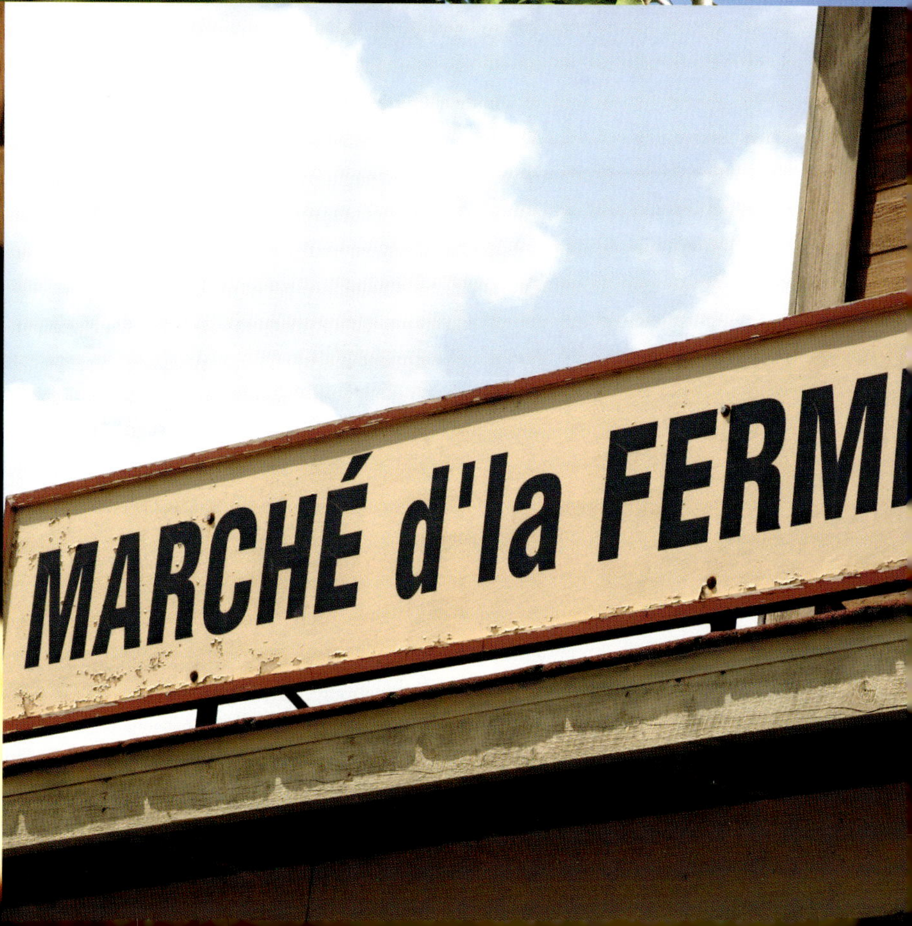
MARCHÉ d'la FERM

Producers (cont.)

Menthe Fraîcheur
Vieille gare de Coaticook
131 rue Lovell
Coaticook
819-849-3256 or 1-866-949-3256
www.menthefraicheur.com

Miellerie Lune de Miel
252 rang 3 Est
Stoke
819-346-2558
www.miellerielunedemiel.com

Moûts de P.O.M. (Les)
819-845-5555

Produits Indigènes
819-839-3881

Verger Le Gros Pierre (Le)
6335 route Louis-St-Laurent
Compton
819-835-5549
www.grospierre.com

Vallons Maraîchers
440 chemin Hyatt's Mills
Compton
819-849-2652

Vignoble de l'Orpailleur (Le)
1086 route 202
Dunham
450-295-2763
www.orpailleur.ca

Vignoble Le Cep d'Argent
1257 chemin de la Rivière
Magog
819-864-4441 or 1-877-864-4441
www.cepdargent.com

Restaurants and Inns

Auberge du Joli Vent
667 chemin Bondville
Lac-Brome
450-243-4272 or 1-866-525-4272
www.aubergedujolivent.com

Auberge Georgeville 1889
71 chemin Channel
Georgeville
819-843-8683
www.aubergegeorgeville.com

Auberge Les Victorines du Lac
1886 route 161 Sud
Lac-Mégantic
819-583-6904 or 1-866-494-6904
www.victorines.qc.ca

Auberge & Spa West Brome
128 route 139
West Brome
450-266-7552 or 1-888-902-7663
www.awb.ca

Bocage (Le)
200 chemin Moe's River
Compton
819-835-5653
www.lebocage.qc.ca

Café Massawippi
3050 chemin Capelton
North Hatley
819-842-4528
www.cafemassawippi.com

Château Bromont (Hôtel)
90 rue Stanstead
Bromont
450-534-3433 or 1-800-304-3433
www.chateaubromont.com

Groupe Germain
www.hotelboutique.com

Hovey Manor
575 chemin Hovey
North Hatley
819-842-2421 or 1-800-661-2421
www.manoirhovey.com

Temps des cerises (Restaurant Le)
79 Du Carmel
Danville
819-839-2818 or 1-800-839-2818
www.cerises.com

Flavours of a Region *Eastern Townships*

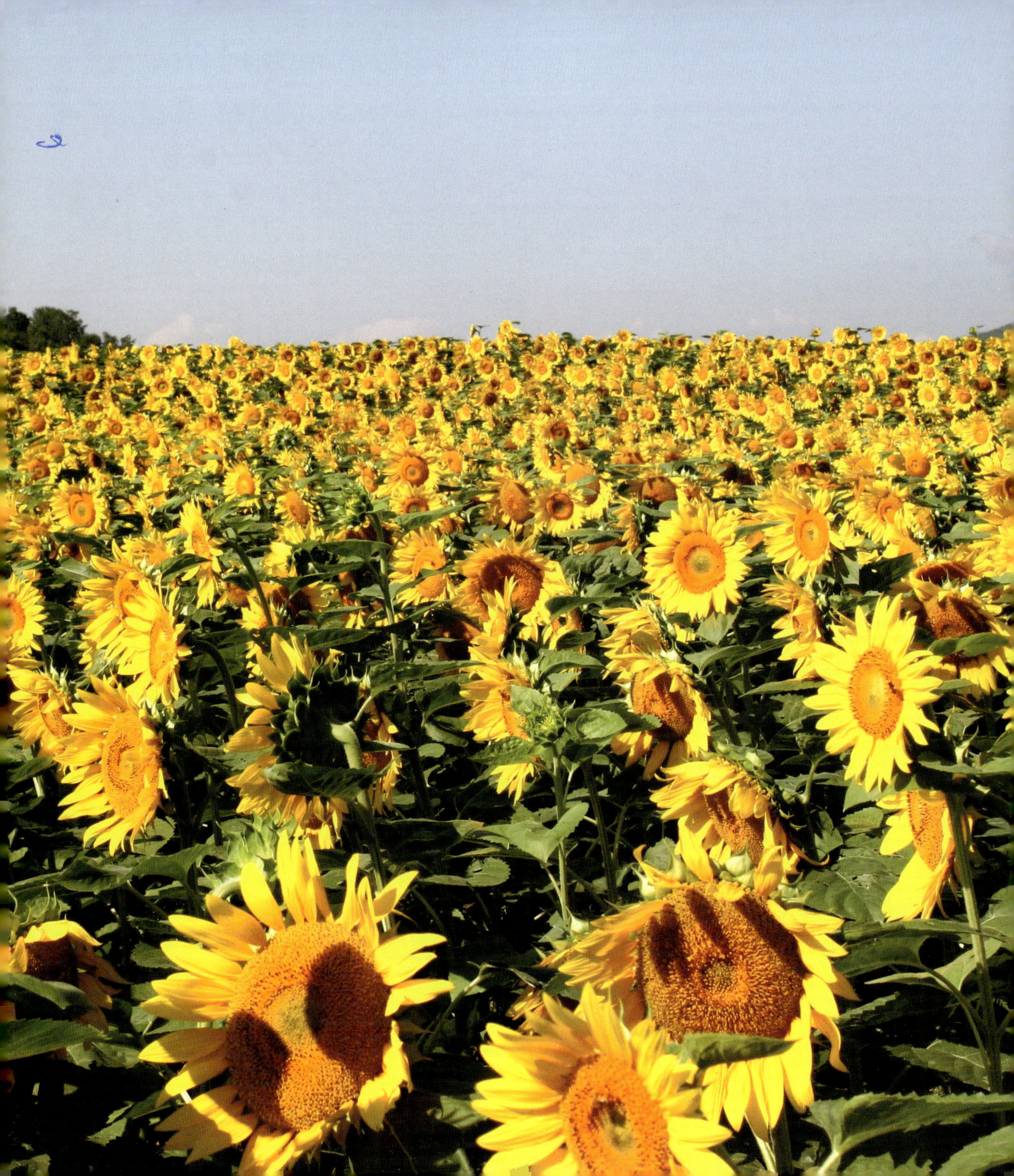